COMMON CORE SUCCESS
LEARN, REVIEW, APPLY

KINDERGARTEN
MATH & ENGLISH LANGUAGE ARTS

Rhonda Shaver & Jennifer Sansivero

Consulting Editors

Copyright © 2015 by Barron's Educational Series, Inc.

All rights reserved.
No part of this publication may be reproduced or distributed in any form
or by any means without the written permission of the copyright owner.

All inquiries should be addressed to:
Barron's Educational Series, Inc.
250 Wireless Boulevard
Hauppauge, NY 11788
www.barronseduc.com

ISBN 978-1-4380-0668-0

Library of Congress Control Number: 2015932524

Date of Manufacture: June 2015
Manufactured by: C&C Offset Printing Co., Ltd, Shenzhen, China

Printed in China

9 8 7 6 5 4 3 2 1

Photo Credits: All photos from Shutterstock except where noted; © Monkey Business Images: pages title (child), 6, 14, 66; © Noka Studios: title page (dots); © Gelpi JM: page 5; © Rawpixel: page 9; © Matthew Cole: pages, 10, 11, 16 (bee), 17 (flower), 23 (moon), (book) 26, 30, 31 (bear), 46 (cow), (frog) 47, 50 (girl), 53 (girl), 55 (boy swimming), 67, 71 (girl), 75 (dove), 80, 84, 93 (left), 128, 167; © paulaphoto: page 12; © Rosa Jay: page 15 (goat); © Ruslan Kudrin: page 15 (coat); © jocic: page 15 (box); © Eric Isselee: page 15 (fox), 159 (seal), page 161 (lion, chimp); © buchan: page 16 (frog); © Big think: page 16 (duck); © Polyudova Yulia: page 16 (truck, tree); © Igor Zakowski: page 16 (dog), 134; © Aeesha Norm: page 17 (sneakers); © zzveillust: page 17 (wagon); © Teguh Mujiono: page 17 (turtle), 72 (hug), 89 (ant); © Sarawut Padungkwan: page 17 (sheep), 87; © smita rudrake: page 17 (squirrel); © Sergei Kolesnikov: page 18; © Pushkin: page 19, 46 (owl), 71 (lamb), 90, 93 (right); © Veronica Louro: page 21; © grmarc: page 22; © Yulia Glam: page 23 (balloon); © pichayasri: page 23 (doll); © HitToon.Com: page 23 (peanut); © udaix: page 23 (mouse); © VIGE.CO: page 23 (door); © Lilu330: page 23 (pony), 48; © AboliC: page 23 (man); © wonlopcolors: page 23 (dress); © Pete Spiro: page 23 (dress); © StockPhotoAstur: page 24; © Studio_G: page 25, 41 (pencil), 95 (pencil); © wavebreakmedia: page 27; © Kakigori Studio: page 28 (vet); © Muhammad Desta Laksana: page 28 (turtle); © Liusa: page 31 (sled); © Juriah Mosin: page 32; © Paket: page 33, 65; © AKIllustration: page 34 (eyes, ears etc.); © Gelpi JM: page 34 (girl), 54 (girl), 86; © Valeriy Lebedev: page 35; © naluwan: page 37; © Proskurina Yuliya: page 42 (earth); © 3445128471: page 42 (boy), 43; © Maxx-Studio: page 45–46 (drums); © Andrea Danti: page 45 (ear); © Albina Tiplyashina: page 45 (clock); © museyushaya: page 46 (baby); © Tatiana Shepeleva: page 46 (train); © Macrovector: page 46 (plane), 72 (bow); © Alina Ku-Ku: page 46 (whistle); © gst: page 46 (light); © omnimoney: page 47 (firetruck); © Lorelyn Medina: page 47 (whisper), 51 (musicians), 73 (cold); © mylisa: page 47 (clock); © creatOR76: page 47 (fireworks); © svkv: page 47 (jackhammer); © paprika: page 47 (dandelions); © Viktorija Reuta: page 47 (horn); 106 (crayon), 143; © nmfotograf: page 47 (birds); © Hayati Kayhan: page 49 (popsicle); © Mega Pixel: page 49 (cocoa); © marmo81: page 49 (pasta); © Studio Barcelona: page 49 (sun), 84 (sun); © Lucy Ya: page 49 (fry pan); © TatjanaRittner: page 49 (fire); © Kraska: page 49 (lightbulb); © Petrov Mykola: page 50 (earth); © Netkoff: page 53 (bowling); © insima: page 53 (duck); © Fotinia: page 53 (necktie); © vector photo video: page 53 (log); © cTermit: page 53 (pen); © bogdan ionescu: page 54 (crayons); © MyClipArtStore.com: page 55 (tent), 58, 59; © Nikolaeva Galina: page 56 (fire, marshmallow); © Christos Georghiou: page 56 (bird); © LoopAll: page 56 (tent); © aekikuis: page 57; © magmarcz: page 60; © Bukhavets Mikhail: page 60 (illustrations), 62; © Natan86: page 61 (paper); © AlexPic: page 63; © Ermolaev Alexander: page 64; © My name is boy: page 69 (horns); © Tom Reichner: page 69 (hoof); © aomnet7: page 69 (fleece); © Sukhonosova Anastasia: page 70; © PinkPueblo: page 71 (school) 138 (ants); © Ann Precious: page 71 (heart); © M.Stasy: page 72 (bell); © Natykach Nataliia: page 72 (cap); © xpixel: page 71 (log); © PILart: page 71 (fish); © Gyvafoto page 73 (umbrella); © Ramona Kaulitzki: page 73 (sun); © Liviu Ionut Pantelimon: page 73 (door); © Tischenko Irina: page 73 (fish, fish tanks); © Armando Camacho M.: page 73 (hot); © tassel78: page 73 (ladybug); © Potapov Alexander: page 75–76 (ant); © DVARG: page 75–76 (dove); © Adya: page 83; © wckiw: (left); © totallyPic.com: page 89 (2); © Bplanet: page 89 (fan); © tawatchai.m: page 89 (hat); © Vitalinka: page 89 (girl); © MidoSemsem: page 89 (boy); © arbit: page 91; © Susan Coons: page 68, 78, 92 (original); © Monkey Business Images: page 95; © Matthias G. Ziegler: page 97; © unien: page 104; © lana rinck: page 106 (ruler, glue, paintbrush, scissors); © Rocket400 Studio: page 106 (pencil, notebook), 165 (notebook, pencil); © inithings: page 106 (marker); © SVIATLANA SHEINA: page 106 (paperclip); © SVIATLANA SHEINA: page 108–109 (fishtanks); © Kate Shannon: page 108 (fish); © Lasha Kilasonia: page 113; © monoo: page 115; © Lykoyanova Juliya: page 118; © Verkhozina Ekaterina: page 119; © daisybee: page 120, 163; © Mirexon: page 122; © best4u: page 126; © www.BillionPhotos.com: page 127; © LAR01JoKa: page 128 (frog); © adriatix: page 136; © Lokichen: page 138–139; © Olesya Kuznetsova: page 140; © Alexander Ryabintsev: page 144–145; © bluebright: page 147; © Martin Bech: page 152 (soup can); © GeorgeMPhotography: page 152 (party hat); © Netfalls – Remy Musser: page 152 (globe); © Planner: page 152 (die); © Z-art: page 153; © Sergey Mikhaylov: page 158; © Alexey V Smirnov: page 159 (igloo); © ILYA AKINSHIN: page 159 (polar bear); © Alexander Kazantsev: page 160 (left); © Charles Brutlag: page 160 (right); © Lightspring: page 161 (butterfly); © gualtiero boffi: page 161 (elephant); © pandapaw: page 161 (zebra); © Ekaterina V. Borisova: page 161 (toucan); © Stannik_fox: page 164; © Swill Klitch: page 165 (sphere); © ILeysen: page 165 (stacked books); © wavebreakmedia: page 170

As of August 2013, 46 states and the District of Columbia had adopted the Common Core State Standards (CCSS) for English Language Arts (ELA) literacy and mathematics. These standards are geared toward preparing students for college, careers, and competition in the global economy. The adoption of the CCSS represents the first time that schools across the nation have had a common set of expectations for what students should know and be able to do. As with any new program, there are growing pains associated with implementation. Teachers are busy adapting classroom materials to meet the standards, and many parents are confused about what the standards mean for their children. As such, it is a prime opportunity for the creation of a workbook series that provides a clear-cut explanation of the standards coupled with effective lessons and activities tied to those standards.

The foundation of Barron's English Language Arts (ELA) literacy and Math workbook for Kindergarten is based on sound educational practices coupled with parent-friendly explanations of the standards and interesting activities for students that meet those standards. While many other workbook series on the market today offer students practice with individual skills outlined in the CCSS, none seem to do so in a cohesive manner. Our goal was to create an exciting series that mirrors the way teachers actually teach in the classroom. Rather than random workbook pages that present each of the CCSS skills in isolation, our series presents the skills in interesting units of related materials that reinforce each of the standards in a meaningful way. We have included Stop and Think (Review/Understand/Discover) sections to assist parents/tutors and students in applying those skills at a higher level. The standards being addressed in each unit are clearly labeled and explained throughout so that parents/tutors have a better grasp of the purpose behind each activity. Additionally, students will be familiar and comfortable with the manner of presentation and learning as this is what they should be accustomed to in their everyday school experiences. These factors will not only assist students in mastering the skills of Kindergarten, but will also provide an opportunity for parents to play a larger role in their children's overall education. Finally, the pedagogical stance of these workbooks will allow Barron's publishing to reach a wider audience. It is our view that it is not only parents and their children who will be able to use these books, but also tutors and teachers!

Lisa Wilson, M.Ed
Amy Owens, NBCT El. Ed

Contents

English Language Arts	6

Reading: Foundational Skills — 13

Unit 1: Learning to Recognize Word Sounds — 15
Understanding Rhyming Words — 15
Understanding Sounds of Syllables — 17
Understanding Onsets and Rimes — 18
Understanding Phonemes in CVC Words — 19
Making New Words — 20

Unit 2: Learning to Recognize Words — 22
Learning Consonant Sounds — 23
Learning Long and Short Vowel Sounds — 24
Recognizing High-Frequency Words — 25
Words that Sound the Same — 26

Unit 3: Fluency: Read with Purpose and Understanding — 27
"My Pet Zet" — 28
Check for Understanding — 29
Guided Questions — 29
"Ted" — 30
Check for Understanding — 31
Guided Questions — 31

Reading and Writing: Informational Texts — 33

Unit 4: All About the Senses — 34
"Your Five Senses" — 35
Learning About the Details — 36
Finding Nouns and Verbs — 37
How to Make Plural Nouns — 38
Using End Punctuation — 39
Learning About Prefixes and Suffixes — 40
Write to Inform — 41

Unit 5: Energy — 42
"Sound Energy" — 43
Main Topic and Key Details — 44
Pictures Help You Understand the Text — 45
Practice Writing Upper- and Lowercase Letters — 46
Sort Objects — 47
"Heat Energy" — 48
Making a Connection — 49
What Are the Parts of a Book? — 50
Compare and Contrast Articles — 51
Prepositions — 52
Words with Many Meanings — 53
Write Your Story — 54
Stop and Think! Units 1–5 — 55
Review — 55
Understand — 59
Discover — 63

Reading and Writing: Literature — 65

Unit 6: Nursery Rhymes and Poetry — 67
"Mary's Lamb" — 67
Understanding the Key Details — 68
Ask Questions About Unknown Words — 69
Recognizing Poems — 70
Practice Writing Upper- and Lowercase Letters — 71
Short Vowel Sounds — 72
Opposite Words — 73
Write Your Opinion — 74

Unit 7: Fables — 75
"The Ant and the Dove" — 76
Main Characters, Settings, and Events — 77
Pictures Help You Understand the Story — 78
Ask Questions About Unknown Words — 79
Recognize Complete and Incomplete Sentences — 80
Using End Punctuation — 81
Using Capital Letters — 81
Understanding Question Words — 82
Become a Good Speller — 83
Real-Life Connections — 85
Shades of Meaning — 86
Stop and Think! Units 6–7 — 87
Review — 87
Understand — 90
Discover — 95

Math	97
Unit 1: CORE Problem-Solving Concepts	**102**
Step 1: Understand	102
Step 2: Identify	103
Step 3: Use a Model to Solve	104
Step 4: Explain Your Thinking	105
Unit 2: CORE Counting and Number Concepts (Numbers 0–10)	**106**
Explore Numbers 1–10	106
Count 0–10	108
How Many?	110
Greater Than–Less Than–Equal To	112
Compare Numbers	114
Unit 3: CORE Counting and Base-Ten Concepts (Numbers 11–19)	**116**
Break Apart Numbers	116
Count 11–19	118
Count On	120
Match Numbers and Names	122
Stop and Think! Units 2–3	124
Review	124
Understand	126
Discover	127
Unit 4: CORE Addition and Subtraction Concepts	**128**
What Is Addition?	128
Practice Adding up to 5	130
Make a Ten	132
What Is Subtraction?	134
Practice Subtracting with Numbers 0–5	136
Unit 5: CORE Counting and Number Set Concepts (Numbers up to 20 and Beyond)	**138**
Count Objects up to 20	138
Count to 50 by Ones	140
Count to 100 by Ones and Tens	142
Stop and Think! Units 4–5	144
Review	144
Understand	146
Discover	147
Unit 6: CORE Geometry Concepts	**148**
Name that Shape	148
Compare Shapes	150
Cylinder, Cone, Sphere, and Cube	152
Build Shapes	154
Where Is It?	156
Unit 7: CORE Measurement and Data Concepts	**158**
Describe Objects	158
Compare Objects	160
Classify Objects	162
Stop and Think! Units 6–7	164
Review	164
Understand	166
Discover	167
Answer Key	**169**

English Language Arts

Common Core Standards for English Language Arts

The following explanation of educational goals is based on the Common Core English Language Arts standards that your child will learn in Kindergarten. A comprehensive list of the Common Core State Standards can be viewed at the following website: *www.corestandards.org*.

Understanding Standard Labels:

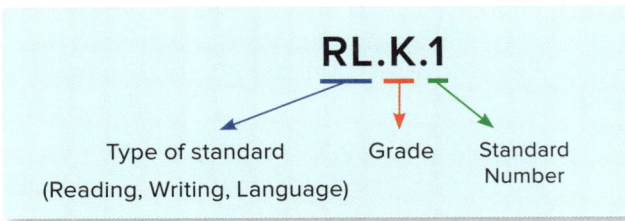

Reading Foundational Skills (RF)

Print Concepts:
(Standards RF.K.1.a–RF.K.1.d)

Your child will do/learn the following:

- Follow words from left to right, top to bottom, and page by page.
- Recognize that spoken words are represented in written language by specific sequences of letters.
- Understand that words are separated by spaces in print.
- Recognize and name all upper- and lowercase letters of the alphabet.

Phonological Awareness:
(Standards RF.K.2.a–RF.K.2.e)

Your child will do/learn the following:

- Recognize and produce rhyming words.
- Count, pronounce, and blend syllables in spoken words.
- Blend and segment onsets and rimes of single-syllable spoken words.
- Isolate and pronounce the initial, medial vowel, and final sounds (phonemes) in three-phoneme (consonant-vowel-consonant or CVC) words.* (This does not include CVCs ending with /l/, /r/, or /x/.)
- Add or substitute individual sounds (phonemes) in simple, one-syllable words to make new words.

Phonics and Word Recognition:
(Standards RF.K.3.a–RF.K.3.d)

Your child will do/learn the following:

- Demonstrate basic knowledge of one-to-one letter-sound correspondences by producing the primary sound or many of the most frequent sounds for each consonant.
- Associate the long and short sounds with common spellings (graphemes) for the five major vowels.
- Read common high-frequency words by sight (e.g., the, of, to, you, she, my, is, are, do, does).
- Distinguish between similarly spelled words by identifying the sounds of the letters that differ.

Fluency:
(Standards RF.K.4)

Your child will do/learn the following:

- Read emergent-reader texts with purpose and understanding.

*Words, syllables, or phonemes written in /slashes/ refer to their pronunciation or phonology. Thus, /CVC/ is a word with three phonemes regardless of the number of letters in the spelling of the word.

Common Core Standards for English Language Arts

Reading Standards
(RI – Reading Informational Text /RL – Reading Literature)

Key Ideas and Details:
(Standards RI.K.1, RI.K.2, RI.K.3, RL.K.1, RL.K.2, RL.K.3)

Your child will do/learn the following:

- With prompting and support, ask and answer questions about key details in a text.
- With prompting and support, identify the main topic and retell key details of a text.
- With prompting and support, describe the connection between two individuals, events, ideas, or pieces of information in a text.
- With prompting and support, ask and answer questions about key details in a text.
- With prompting and support, retell familiar stories, including key details.
- With prompting and support, identify characters, setting, and major events in a story.

Craft and Structure:
(Standards RI.K.4, RI.K.5, RI.K.6, RL.K.4, RL.K.5, RL.K.6)

Your child will do/learn the following:

- With prompting and support, ask and answer questions about unknown words in a text.
- Identify the front cover, back cover, and title page of a book.
- Name the author and illustrator of a text and define the role of each in presenting ideas or information in a text.
- Ask and answer questions about unknown words in a text.
- Recognize common types of texts (e.g., storybooks, poems)
- With prompting and support, name the author and illustrator of a story and define the role of each in telling the story.

Integration of Knowledge and Ideas:
(Standards RI.K.7, RI.K.8, RI.K.9, RL.K.7, RL.K.9)

Your child will do/learn the following:

- With prompting and support, describe the relationship between illustrations and the text in which they appear (e.g., what person, place, thing, or idea in the text an illustration depicts).
- With prompting and support, identify the reasons an author gives to support points in a text.
- With prompting and support, identify basic similarities in and differences between two texts on the same topic (e.g., in illustrations, descriptions, or procedures).
- With prompting and support, describe the relationship between illustrations and the story in which they appear (e.g., what moment in a story an illustration depicts).
- With prompting and support, compare and contrast the adventures and experiences of characters in familiar stories.

Writing Standards (W)

Text Types and Purposes:
(Standards W.K.1, W.K.2, W.K.3)

Your child will do/learn the following:

- Use a combination of drawing, dictating, and writing to compose opinion pieces in which they tell a reader the topic and name of the book they are writing about and state an opinion or preference about the topic of book (e.g., My favorite book is . . .).
- Use a combination of drawing, dictating, and writing to compose informative/explanatory texts in which they name what they are writing about and supply some information about the topic.
- Use a combination of drawing, dictating, and writing to narrate a single event or several loosely linked events, tell about the events in the order in which they occurred, and provide a reaction to what happened.

Production and Distribution of Writing:
(Standards W.K.5 and W.K.6)

With the help of an adult or peer, your child will do/learn the following:

- Respond to questions and suggestions from peers and add details to strengthen writing as needed.
- Explore a variety of digital tools to produce and publish writing, including in collaboration with peers.

Common Core Standards for English Language Arts

Research to Build and Present Knowledge:
(Standards W.K.7 and W.K.8)

Your child will do/learn the following:

- Participate in shared research and writing projects (e.g., explore a number of books by a favorite author and express opinions about them).
- With guidance and support from adults, recall information from experiences or gather information from provided sources to answer a question.

Language Standards (L)

Conventions of Standard English:
(Standards L.K.1.a–L.K.1.f and L.K.2.a–L.K.2.d)

Your child will do/learn the following:

- Print many upper- and lowercase letters.
- Use frequently occurring nouns and verbs.
- Form regular plural nouns orally by adding /s/ or /es/ (e.g., dog, dogs; wish, wishes).
- Understand and use question words (interrogatives) (e.g., who, what, where, when, why, how).
- Use the most frequently occurring prepositions (e.g., to, from, in, out, on, off, for, of, by, with).
- Produce and expand complete sentences in shared language activities.

Vocabulary Acquisition and Use:
(Standards L.K.4.a–L.K.4.b, L.K.5.a–L.K.5.d, and L.K.6)

With the help of an adult or peer, your child will do/learn the following:

- Identify new meaning for familiar words and apply them accurately (e.g., knowing a duck is a bird and learning the verb to duck).
- Use most frequently occurring inflections and affixes (e.g., -ed, -s, re-, un-, pre-, -ful, -less) as a clue to the meaning of an unknown word.
- Sort common objects into categories (e.g., shapes, foods) to gain a sense of the concepts the categories represent.
- Demonstrate understanding or frequently occurring verbs and adjectives by relating them to their opposites (antonyms).
- Identify real-life connections between words and their use (e.g., note places at school that are colorful).
- Distinguish shades of meaning among verbs describing the same general action (e.g., walk, march, strut, prance) by acting out the meanings.

Aa
A is for ant.

Bb
B is for bus.

Cc
C is for cow.

Gg
G is for goat.

Hh
H is for hat.

Ii
I is for ink.

Mm
M is for moon.

Nn
N is for net.

Oo
O is for owl.

Ss
S is for sun.

Tt
T is for toys.

Uu
U is for up.

Yy
Y is for yak.

Zz
Z is for zoo.

Dd
D is for dog.

Ee
E is for eye.

Ff
F is for fox.

Jj
J is for jam.

Kk
K is for kite.

Ll
L is for lion.

Pp
P is for pig.

Qq
Q is for queen.

Rr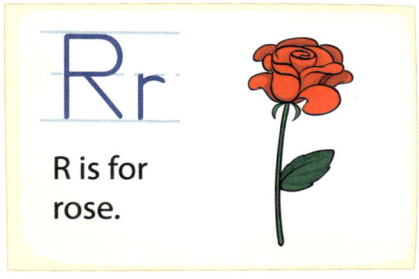
R is for rose.

Vv
V is for van.

Ww
W is for wave.

Xx
X is for xylophone.

my alphabet

Reading: Foundational Skills

Adults: Use this book to assist your emerging reader. Help your student apply the reading strategies to decode and recognize new words. Help him or her to build vocabulary by memorizing and identifying high-frequency words. With prompting and support, your student will excel in his or her reading abilities.

Learning to Recognize Word Sounds

UNIT 1

UNDERSTANDING RHYMING WORDS

Do you know any songs? Many songs have words that rhyme. Words that rhyme sound the same at the end. Here are some words that rhyme!

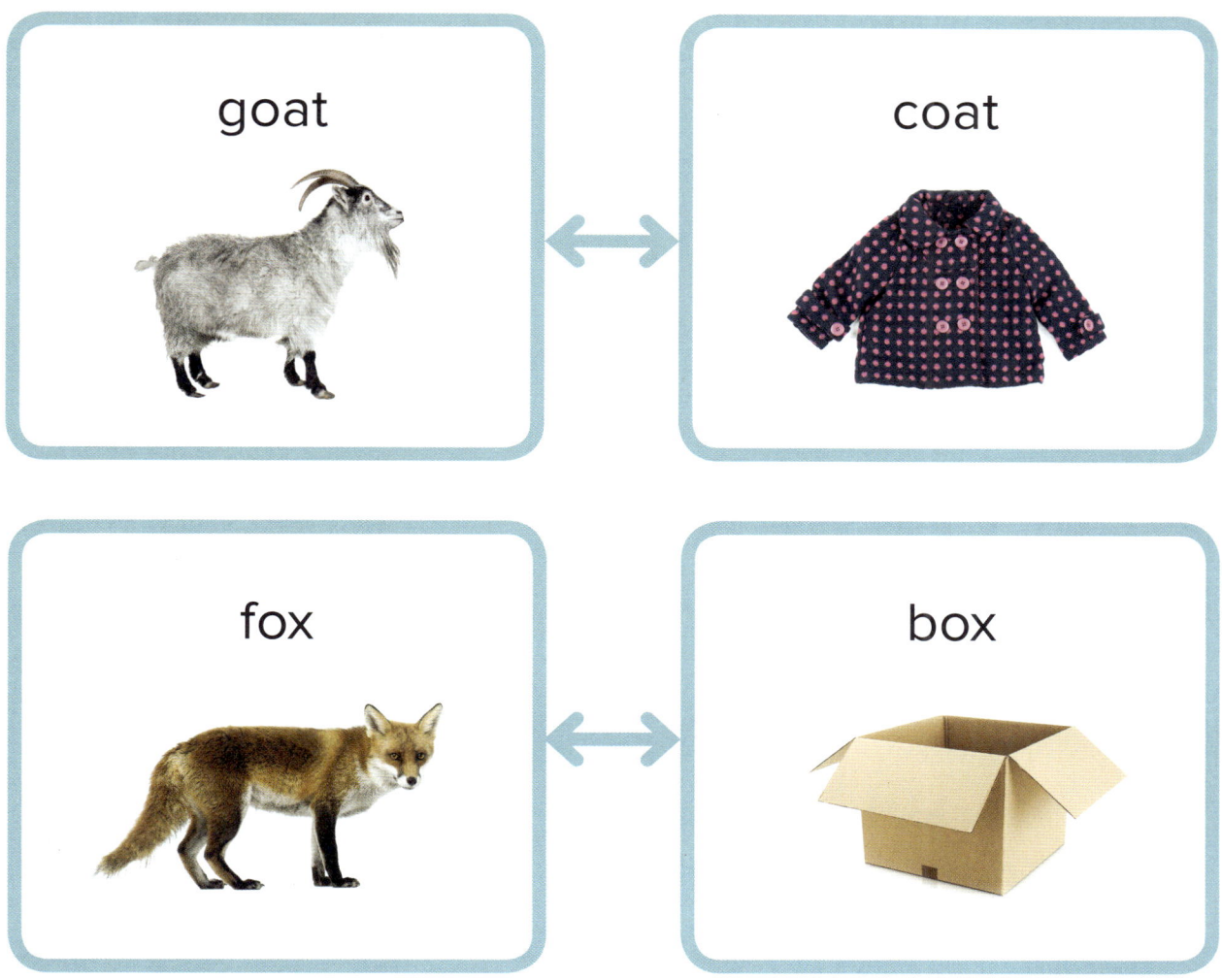

Reading: Foundational Skills

Activity 1

Draw a line to connect the words that rhyme.

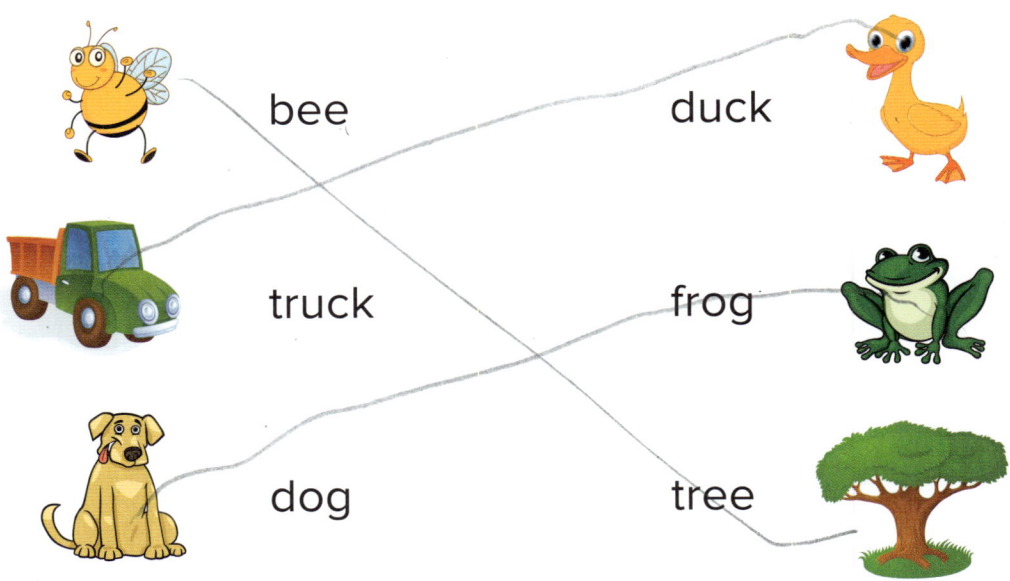

bee — duck

truck — frog

dog — tree

Activity 2

Circle the correct word that makes each sentence rhyme.

1. I have fun in the _____.   sun /(pool)

2. We will bake a tasty _____.   pie /(cake)

3. The little boy played with a _____.   ball /(toy)

Activity 3

Circle the words in the sentence that rhyme.

Pete's (pet) got (wet).

16   Standard RF.K.2.a

Unit 1: Learning to Recognize Word Sounds

UNDERSTANDING SOUNDS OF SYLLABLES

A **syllable** (sill-la-bull) always has one vowel sound. Some words have many vowel sounds.

Say the word *monkey*. How many vowel sounds does the word monkey have?

monkey ⇢ mun + kee = 2 vowel sounds

Activity 1

Circle the words that have two syllable sounds.

 shoes    flower    wagon

Activity 2

How many syllables does each word have? Write the number of syllables next to each word.

 turtle _____

 sheep _____

 squirrel _____

Reading: Foundational Skills

UNDERSTANDING ONSETS AND RIMES

One-syllable words begin with a sound called the onset. Many words begin with the same onset sounds. Sometimes two consonants can make an onset sound.

br	bring	Marco will bring a toy to the party.
pl	play	We will play a game tomorrow.
st	story	The story was about three pigs.

One-syllable words end with a sound called the rime. These words have the same rime sound.

nest	best
fall	tall
hit	fit

Activity 1

Use the word bank to complete each word.

A. _____ _____ e p

B. _____ _____ a p

C. _____ _____ u m

word bank fl   dr   st

Activity 2

Match the words with the same rime sound.

bad	kiss
fish	sad
miss	wish

Unit 1: Learning to Recognize Word Sounds

UNDERSTANDING PHONEMES IN CVC WORDS

CVC means consonant-vowel-consonant. A CVC word is like a cookie with a cream filling in the center. The two hard cookie shells are the consonants. The vowel is like the cream center that holds the consonants together. Some CVC words have three phonemes in them. This means the word makes three sounds.

Phoneme (foh-neem) may look like a strange word, but you speak phonemes every time you talk! A phoneme is the shortest sound in a word. For example, say the word *cat* very slowly. The word *cat* has three phonemes.

cat ⇢ /k/ /a/ /t/

The "**c**" makes the first sound /k/.

The "**a**" makes the second sound /a/.

The "**t**" makes the last sound /t/.

Now say the word **cat** quickly. Can you hear the different phonemes?

Activity 1

Read the sentence.

   I <u>ran</u> down the street.

Circle the phoneme to complete the word *ran*: /r/ /____/ /n/?

   A. a

   B. u

   C. o

Standard RF.K.2.d

Reading: Foundational Skills

Activity 2

Adults: Have your student say the sound of each letter. Then ask your student to match the phonemes to the correct word.

/b/ /u/ /s/   hen

/k/ /a/ /p/   bus

/h/ /e/ /n/   cap

MAKING NEW WORDS

Words are made of letters. Each letter has a sound. One or more letters can make a sound called a phoneme (foh-neem). A phoneme is the shortest sound in a word.

It is easy to change a phoneme sound in a word. Just change one letter to a new letter. The new letter will make a new phoneme sound. This is how to make new words!

Read the phonemes in the word *pat*.

pat ⇢ /p/ /a/ /t/

What happens if you take away the /p/ sound?

/a/ /t/ − /p/ ⇢ /a/ /t/ ⇢ at

Now add phoneme /s/ in front of the phonemes /a/ and /t/:

/s/ + /a/ /t/ ⇢ sat

You have made the word *sat*!

Unit 1: Learning to Recognize Word Sounds

Activity 1

Read the word.

tug

Circle letters you can use instead of "t" to make a new word.

b   f   h   n   r   w

Write the new words using the letters you circled.

A. ____ u g

B. ____ u g

C. ____ u g

Activity 2

1. Read the word.

   f <u>a</u> n

   Which letter is underlined? _____

2. Change the underlined letter to a new letter to make a new word. Which letter should you use?

   A.   e

   B.   o

   C.   u

3. What is the new word? _____

UNIT 2
Learning to Recognize Words

Adults, you can help your student make progress in reading by encouraging him or her to learn **sight words**. Also called **high-frequency words**, these words occur regularly in many texts that students read. They are not always easy to sound out, so it is good to have your student commit these words to memory.

Make learning fun. Sing songs, tell funny stories, and play games as you help your students remember these words.

Sight Words

about	every	make	their	was
are	from	my	then	went
around	have	one	there	were
because	know	play	they	when
could	like	said	very	with
down	little	some	want	would

Standard RF.K.3

Unit 2: Learning to Recognize Words

LEARNING CONSONANT SOUNDS

Most of the letters in the alphabet are consonants. They all have different sounds. Many words begin with the same consonant sound. Say each letter out loud. Then say the word next to it.

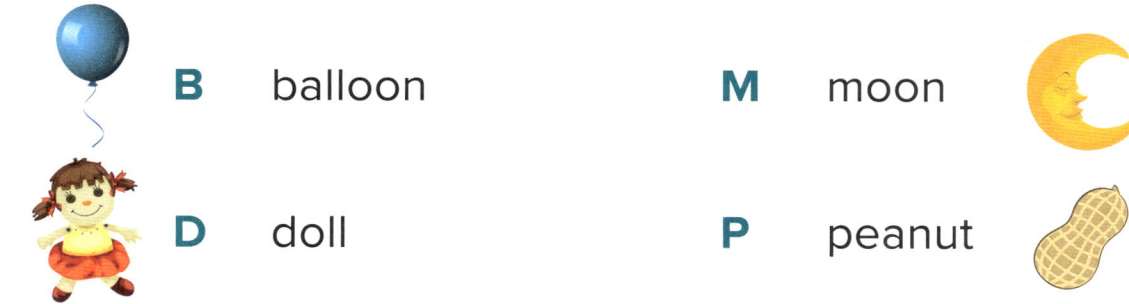

B balloon   **M** moon

D doll   **P** peanut

Activity 1

Match the pictures that begin with the same consonant sound.

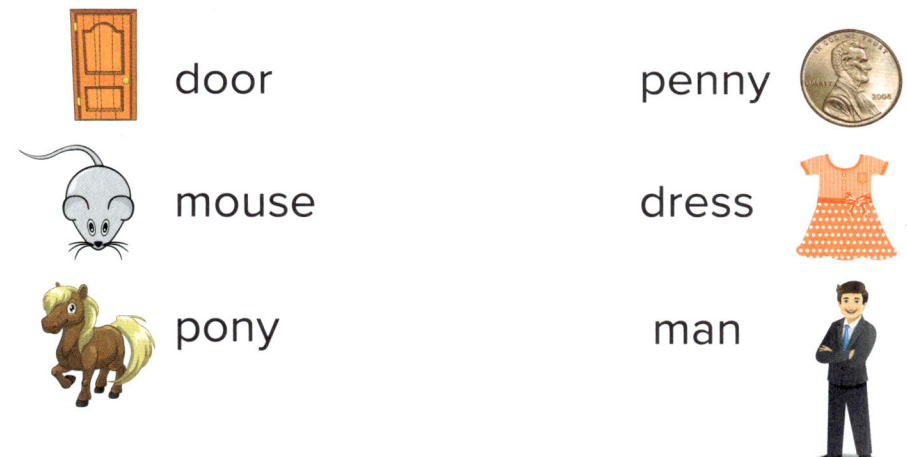

door   penny

mouse   dress

pony   man

Activity 2

Circle all the words that begin with the same sound as book.

The boy found a basketful of furry bunnies.

Standard RF.K.3.a

Reading: Foundational Skills

LEARNING LONG AND SHORT VOWEL SOUNDS

The alphabet has many letters. Five letters are very special. These letters are **a**, **e**, **i**, **o**, **u**. They are called vowels. Every word has one or more vowels. Some words have only one vowel sound.

Some vowels make long sounds in words.

A	name	My n**a**me is Tina.
E	she	Sh**e** ate an apple.
I	night	The n**i**ght was dark.
O	no	Farrah had n**o** bananas.
U	tune	Max sang a t**u**ne.

Some vowels make short sounds in words.

A	tag	The shirt had a t**a**g on it.
E	pet	Miko had a p**e**t hamster.
I	hit	Travis h**i**t the ball with a bat.
O	pot	Kayla cooked dinner in a p**o**t.
U	bug	The b**u**g crawled up the tree.

Activity 1

Circle the word with the short vowel sound.

A. if

B. we

C. oh

Standard RF.K.3.b

Unit 2: Learning to Recognize Words

RECOGNIZING HIGH-FREQUENCY WORDS

As discussed in the beginning of this unit, there are some words you read and speak all the time. These words are called high-frequency (hi-free-kwin-see) words. Sometimes these words are not easy to sound out. Take the time to remember these words, the sounds they make, and the letters that spell them.

Read the words in the word bank. Do you hear these words a lot? Do you use them, too?

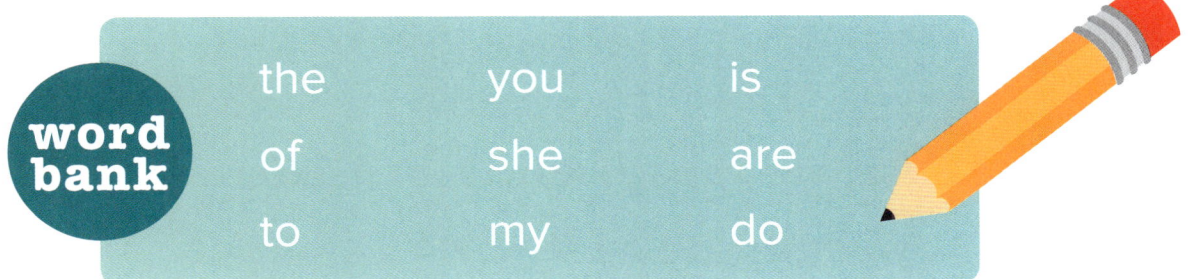

word bank: the, you, is, of, she, are, to, my, do

Activity 1

Circle three high-frequency words in the sentence.

What book are you going to read next?

Activity 2

Circle the correct word to finish the sentence.

I will wash _____ (do/my) face before bedtime.

_____ (The/She) puppy wagged its tail.

Titus _____ (of/is) playing a game.

Standard RF.K.3.c

Reading: Foundational Skills

WORDS THAT SOUND THE SAME

Some words share the same letters. These words may have only one consonant or vowel that makes it sound different.

Sometimes a vowel makes a word sound different. Read the words below. Which letter makes them sound different?

        pat   pet   put

Sometimes a consonant can make a word sound different. Read the words below. Which letter makes them sound different?

        ball   fall   call

Activity 1

Circle the letter that makes each word sound different.

    A.   wish   wash

    B.   had   hid

    C.   step   stop

Activity 2

Use the word bank to answer the question.

| c | g | l | m | r | **word bank** |

Fill in the blank to make a new word.

    A.   ____ e t

    B.   ____ e t

    C.   ____ e t

Fluency: Read with Purpose and Understanding

UNIT 3

Now you will practice reading with an adult. You do not have to know all of the words right now. Recognize and say as many words as you can. Remember to use the following strategies:

- Read the title and think of the story
- Look at the picture clues
- Start the word—say the beginning sounds
- Look for familiar parts in a word
- Reread to improve understanding and/or to improve fluency
- Read ahead and use the words after to help you figure out the unknown word

My Pet Zet

I have a turtle for a pet.

His name is Zet.

Zet is wet.

He is stuck in a net.

Zet needs a vet.

Here comes the vet.

She comes on a jet.

She will help Zet.

Zet met the vet.

The vet likes Zet.

Zet likes the vet.

The vet took off the net.

The vet helped Zet.

You know what I bet?

Zet will not play with a net!

Unit 3: Fluency

CHECK FOR UNDERSTANDING

Adults, after your student has finished reading, ask him or her to provide a brief summary of the story. This will let you know if he or she understood what was read. Write what your student says on the lines below.

_____
_____
_____
_____

GUIDED QUESTIONS

Use "My Pet Zet" to answer the following questions.

1. Why does Zet need a vet?

    A. He is wet.

    B. He made a bet.

    C. He is stuck in a net.

2. Who helps Zet?

    _____

3. Draw a picture of Zet stuck in a net.

Standard RF.K.4

Ted

My name is Ned.

I have a bear.

His name is Ted.

He likes to ride on my red sled.

One day, Ted fell off and hit his head.

"Help! I fear that Ted is dead!"

I ran to get help from Dr. Jed.

"Help!" I said to Dr. Jed.

"Today my bear fell off my sled.

Now, I fear that he is dead!"

Dr. Jed and I—to Ted we fled.

Then Dr. Jed looked down at Ted,

and this is what Dr. Jed said,

"Ted may have a bump on his head.

But he is not dead!"

"Take Ted home and put him to bed!"

Unit 3: Fluency

CHECK FOR UNDERSTANDING

Adults, after your student has finished reading, ask him or her to provide a brief summary of the story. This will let you know if he or she understood what was read. Write what your student says on the lines below.

_____
_____
_____
_____

GUIDED QUESTIONS

Use "Ted" to answer the following questions.

1. Who is Ted?

    A. A boy

    B. A doctor

    C. A bear

2. How did Ted hit his head?

    A. Ted fell out of bed.

    B. Ted fell off a sled.

    C. Ted fell off a bike.

3. What does the doctor tell Ned to do with Ted?

    A. Take him to Jed's.

    B. Let him ride on the sled.

    C. Put him to bed.

Reading and Writing: Informational Texts

UNIT 4
All About the Senses

Having five senses helps you to enjoy many things about life. In this unit, you will learn interesting facts about the wonderful things your eyes, ears, nose, tongue, and skin can do.

sight

hearing

taste

smell

touch

Unit 4: All About the Senses

Your Five Senses

You can see a pretty rainbow with your eyes. You can hear a loud train with your ears. You can smell a yummy pie baking with your nose. You can taste a sweet orange with your tongue. Your fingers can touch a soft bunny rabbit.

To do all of this, you use your five senses.

You use your **sense** of sight to see. Your eyes work like a **camera**. They take pictures. They send the pictures to your brain. Your brain tells you what you see.

You use your sense of hearing to hear. Your ears give the message to your brain. The sounds may be loud, or low. Your brain tells you what you heard.

You use your sense of smell to smell. Smells float through the air to your nose. Your nose sends the message to your brain. Your brain tells you what you smell.

You use your sense of taste to enjoy food. Your tongue has tiny **taste buds**. Taste buds tell your brain about what you eat. Your brain tells you what you taste.

You use your sense of touch to feel. Special cells in your skin send **information** to your brain. Your brain tells you what it felt like.

glossary

Camera: A machine that is used for taking pictures or for making movies.

Information: Facts or details about something.

Sense: One of the five natural powers (touch, taste, smell, sight, and hearing) through which you receive information.

Taste buds: One of many small spots on your tongue that give you the ability to taste things.

Reading and Writing: Informational Texts

LEARNING ABOUT THE DETAILS

Use "Your Five Senses" to answer the questions below.

1. Which two of your five senses do you use to watch your favorite movie?

   _____

   _____

2. How are your eyes the same as a camera?

   A. They both see a rainbow.
   B. They both take pictures.
   C. They both send pictures to the brain.

When an author writes, he or she must include **details** to support the points made in the text. Sometimes, these details connect to each other, helping you to understand the points more clearly.

3. Put these events in order. Place a 1, 2, or 3 on the lines.

   _____ Your nose sends messages about what you smell to your brain.

   _____ Your brain tells you what you smell.

   _____ Smells float through the air to your nose.

4. Which sentence tells the reason why you can hear?

   A. You use your sense of hearing to hear.
   B. You can hear a loud train with your ears.
   C. Your ears give the message to your brain.

Unit 4: All About the Senses

FINDING NOUNS AND VERBS

A **noun** is a person, place, or thing. **Verbs** are words that show action. Verbs tell what the noun is doing.

Activity 1

Circle the verb and underline the noun in the sentences below.

1. I hear a dog.
2. I see a fish.
3. I feel the sun.
4. I smell a flower.

Activity 2

Write a noun and a verb. Use them in a sentence.

1. Noun: _____

    Verb: _____

    Your sentence: _____

    _____

    _____

    _____

Standard L.K.1.b

Reading and Writing: Informational Texts

HOW TO MAKE PLURAL NOUNS

When a noun names more than one person, place, or thing, it becomes a **plural noun**. Plural nouns often end in **s** or **es**.

> You add an **s** to a regular noun
>
> *Examples:* I like to watch the bird make a nest.
> I like to watch the **birds** make their nest.
>
> You add **es** to nouns that end in ch, sh, s, x, or z.
>
> *Examples:* I put my dish in the sink.
> I put my **dishes** in the sink.

Activity 1

Add *s* or *es* to make each word below plural.

1. fox _____
2. train _____
3. boy _____
4. potato _____

Activity 2

Complete the chart. Write the singular or plural form of each noun.

Singular	Plural
bush	
	benches
nose	
	fleas

Standard L.K.1.c

Unit 4: All About the Senses

USING END PUNCTUATION

There are three types of punctuation that end sentences: **period (.)**, **question mark (?)**, and **exclamation point (!)**.

A **period (.)** is used at the end of a sentence that tells something.

A **question mark (?)** is used at the end of a sentence that is asking you something.

An **exclamation point (!)** is used at the end of a sentence that shows excitement.

Examples:
I had eggs for breakfast. (telling sentence)
Did you have homework last night? (asking sentence)
I made the team! (excited sentence)

Place the correct punctuation (. ? or !) at the end of each sentence.

1. Do you like the taste of spicy food ____

2. We saw a flock of geese on the pond ____

3. What is that stinky smell ____

4. Look, out there's a tiger behind you ____

Standard L.K.2.b

Reading and Writing: Informational Texts

LEARNING ABOUT PREFIXES AND SUFFIXES

To understand the meaning of a word, divide the word into its parts.

1. **undone = un + done**
   un means not / done means finished
   undone = something that is not finished

2. **helpful = help + ful**
   help means to give support / ful means full of
   helpful = giving full support

3. **walked = walk + ed**
   walk means to move your legs / ed is past tense; it happened already
   walked = you already moved your legs

Choose a suffix or a prefix to complete each sentence below.

Prefix	Meaning	Suffix	Meaning
un	not	ful	full of
re	again	ed	past tense

1. I fell because my shoes were ____tied.

2. Let's ____read the book to understand it better.

3. You can have fun with my puppy because he is very play____.

4. The boy cleaned up the mess after he spill____ the milk.

Unit 4: All About the Senses

WRITE TO INFORM

When you write to inform, you tell your audience about topics that they may not know too much about.

The article says your eyes are like a camera. List two reasons that show they are. Draw a picture to support your explanation.

UNIT 5

Energy

Energy is the ability to do work. It comes in different forms. Some of these forms are heat, sound, and light energy. Let's learn about the different kinds of energy that you use every day. Listen as your adult helper reads the story to you.

Sound Energy

Snap your fingers. Stomp your feet. Sing a happy song. How are these different sounds made?

Sound is energy made from **vibrations**. Energy is the **ability** to move or do work. When an object vibrates, it moves back and forth. The air parts around it to bump into other air parts. This movement, called **sound waves**, keeps going until the energy runs out. If you are near, you will hear the sound.

When a drummer beats a drum, sound waves **travel** in the air. Afterward, the sound waves reach your ears. How does this happen?

Picture yourself in a pool. You are at one end of the pool playing with your toys. Your friend is at the other end. As you play, you create waves that move in the water. The waves get bigger and bigger. Finally, the waves reach your friend at the other end of the pool. The same is true with sound.

When vibrations are fast, more sound waves are made. The sound will be high. When vibrations are slow, fewer sound waves are made. The sound will be low. A baby's cry is a high sound. The clap of thunder is a low sound. Big sound waves make loud sounds. Small sound waves make soft sounds.

Now you know how sound is made! Tell a friend about what you have learned.

Reading and Writing: Informational Texts

glossary

Ability: Having the power to do something.

Vibrations: Steady shaking movements.

Sound wave: A wave that moves through the air and carries the sound to your ear.

Travel: Moving from one place to another.

MAIN TOPIC AND KEY DETAILS

Use "Sound Energy" to answer the following questions.

1. What is the main topic of the passage?
   A. High and low sounds
   B. How sound is made
   C. Making pool waves

The **main topic** is what the text is mostly about. The other sentences are the key details that tell more about the main topic.

2. Fast vibrations make _____ sounds.
   A. loud   B. soft   C. high

3. Slow vibrations make _____ sounds.
   A. soft   B. low   C. high

4. What kind of sound does thunder make?
   A. high   B. low   C. soft

Unit 5: Energy

PICTURES HELP YOU UNDERSTAND THE TEXT

Pictures can help you to see more clearly the different things the author speaks about in the text. Sometimes, a picture can show the same things as reading many words.

Use "Sound Energy" to answer the following questions.

1. What does this picture show?

   _____

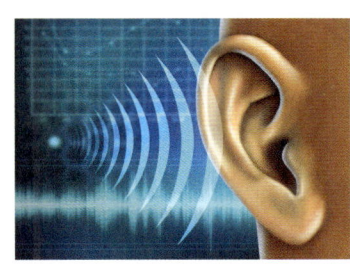

2. Underline the sentence that matches the picture.

   A. The sound waves reach your ears.

   B. The sound will be high.

3. Underline the sentence that matches the picture.

   A. We hear loud sounds.

   B. We hear soft sounds.

Digging Deeper

Make Your Own Phone!

Adults: Try this fun experiment with your student. Each person gets a paper cup. Stand across the room from your partner. Quietly take turns speaking into the cups. Can you hear your partner? Now try this. Poke holes in the bottom of each cup. Add one piece of string to connect both of the cups. Attach a paper clip to prevent the string from going back through the hole. Go back and stand across from your partner. Pull the string tight. Now take turns speaking into the cups. What do you notice this time? Is there a difference? When you speak into the cup, the bottom of the cup vibrates and the string carries the sound to the other cup!

Standard RI.K.7

45

Reading and Writing: Informational Texts

PRACTICE WRITING UPPER- AND LOWERCASE LETTERS

Say the name of each picture. Write the first letter of each picture in both uppercase and lowercase letters. Then circle the pictures of things that make high sounds.

Unit 5: Energy

SORT OBJECTS

Circle the pictures of things that make loud sounds.

A fire engine siren

A child whispering

A clock ticking

Firecrackers

A man using a jackhammer

A gentle breeze

A horn

A bird chirping

Heat Energy

The sun keeps us warm and gives us light. Without it, the Earth would be **frozen**. Heat energy from the sun keeps the Earth and all of the things on it alive.

Heat is the giving of energy from one substance or body to another. You cannot see heat energy. But you know it is there. On a hot day, you feel heat from the sun. It makes you warm. Heat travels from the sun to Earth by **radiation**.

Another way to feel heat is to touch something hot. If you walk on hot sand at the beach, you will feel heat. When this happens, it is called **conduction**. The sand is conducting heat to your feet, causing them to burn. But the sand does not make the heat. The sun radiates heat waves to the sand until it becomes hot.

The sun is not the only thing that can make heat. Your body also makes heat. What happens when you are cold? You may shake and shiver. When you shiver, your muscles **tighten** and **relax** quickly. By doing this, your body makes heat. Your body can also make heat when you move. So if you are cold, keep your body moving!

glossary

Conduction: To transfer heat through something such as water or metal.

Frozen: To become a hard substance (such as ice) because of cold.

Radiation: The process of giving off energy in the form of waves or rays.

Tighten: To become stiff.

Relax: To become less stiff.

Unit 5: Energy

MAKING A CONNECTION

Use "Heat Energy" to answer the following questions.

1. How is your body like the sun?
   _____

2. If you cannot see heat, how do you know it is there?

   A. I can feel things that are warm.
   B. I can read books about things that are hot.
   C. I can look at the sun and know heat is there.

3. Put a check mark next to the picture that shows something frozen.

Circle the pictures of things that conduct heat that you can touch. Underline the pictures of things that radiate heat by waves that you cannot see or touch.

Standards RI.K.1, RI.K.3, RI.K.4

Reading and Writing: Informational Texts

WHAT ARE THE PARTS OF A BOOK?

Look at each of the pictures.

Tell if the picture is the front cover, the back cover, or the title page of the book. Write your answer on the lines below.

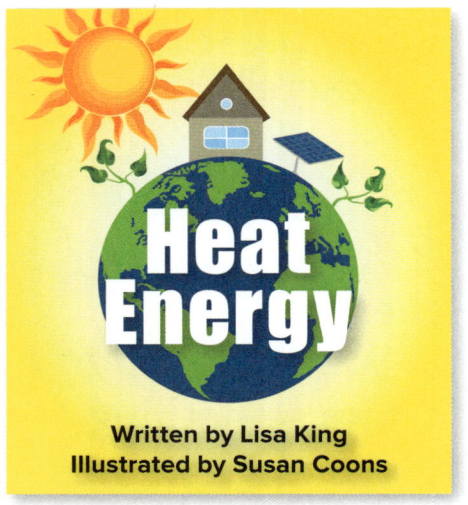 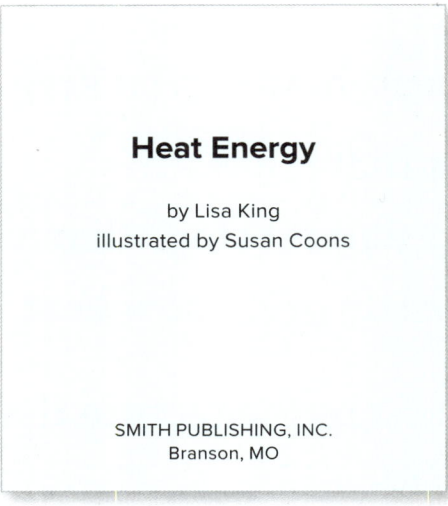 

_____   _____   _____

1. Who wrote the book "Heat Energy?"

   _____

2. Who drew the pictures for the book "Heat Energy?"

   _____

Unit 5: Energy

COMPARE AND CONTRAST ARTICLES

How are the passages "Sound Energy" and "Heat Energy" alike? How are they different? Answer these questions by filling in the Venn diagram.

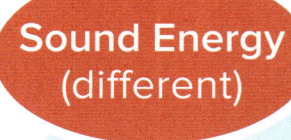

Standard RI.K.9

Reading and Writing: Informational Texts

PREPOSITIONS

A **preposition** is a word that shows the relationship between a noun or a pronoun and another word in the sentence.

> The word **on** is the preposition; it shows the relationship between the pen and the book.
>
> > My pen is **on** the book.
>
> A helpful hint to remember is that prepositions tell location. If the preposition changes, the location of the pen in relation to the book also changes.
>
> > My pen is **under** the book.
> >
> > My pen is **in** the book.
>
> A preposition can also show when something happens.
>
> > Ben **always** plays with his dog.
>
> The word **always** is the preposition. It tells us when Ben plays with his dog. Now let's change the preposition in this sentence. The meaning will also change.
>
> > Ben **never** plays with his dog.
> >
> > Ben **rarely** plays with his dog.

Choose the correct preposition from the word bank to complete the sentences below.

1. The sun is _____ the sky.
2. The clock is _____ the wall.
3. Don't fall _____ the stairs.
4. The man is walking _____ the shore.

word bank
- on
- down
- along
- in

Standard L.K.1.e

Unit 5: Energy

WORDS WITH MANY MEANINGS

Words can have more than one meaning. These are **multiple-meaning** words.

Circle the sentence that matches the picture.

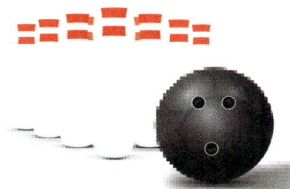

Do you like to **bowl**?

Can I have a **bowl** of soup?

You better **duck**!

The **duck** is pretty.

My dad wears a **tie**.

The game ended in a **tie**.

Tree **bark** is rough.

The dog likes to **bark**.

She **saw** a bug.

We use a **saw** to cut wood.

We write with a **pen**.

The pig lives in a **pen**.

Standard L.K.4.a

Reading and Writing: Informational Texts

WRITE YOUR STORY

When did you first learn what the word *hot* meant? Did you touch something hot? Did you feel the heat from a warm fire? Was it a good or bad experience? Describe how you first learned about heat. Make it into a nice story.

To begin, think about the following:

1. What is your event?
2. Describe what happened in the order in which the events occurred.
3. How did you react to the event?

Draw a picture to illustrate your story.

REVIEW

Congratulations! You have completed the lessons in Units 1–5. Now you will have the opportunity to practice some of the skills you just learned.

Reading Fluency

Camping Is Fun

Camping is fun!
I help dad put up our tent.
I hear a boat.
I can ride in a boat.
I see a lake.
I can swim in the lake.
I smell smoke.
I can sit by the fire.
I eat hot dogs.
They taste good!
I get in the tent.
I get under the covers.
I feel warm.
I can see the moon.
Goodnight, moon!

Units 1–5 Stop and Think! Review

Activity 1

Say the name of each picture. Write the first letter of each picture in both uppercase and lowercase letters.

   Upper   Lower   Upper   Lower

   Upper   Lower   Upper   Lower

Adults: Reading can be a fun journey. As you help your student learn to read, remember to have your student do the following:

- Read the title and think of the story
- Look at the picture clues
- Start the word—say the beginning sounds
- Look for familiar parts in a word
- Reread to improve understanding and/or to improve fluency
- Read ahead and use the words after to help you figure out the unknown

These strategies will help your student successfully read and understand even challenging passages.

Stop and Think! Review   Units 1–5

Activity 2

Look at the pictures. Fill in the blanks with the prepositions from the word bank.

word bank between   around   front   through   behind

1. The owl is standing in _____ of the box.
2. The owl is standing _____ the box.
3. The owl is standing _____ the two boxes.
4. The owl is flying _____ the pole.
5. The owl is going _____ the hole in the box.

Activity 3

Underline all the prepositions in "Camping Is Fun."
(*Hint:* There are 5.)

Units 1–5 Stop and Think! Review

Activity 4

Draw a square around the things you get inside of.
Draw a circle around the things that help you to see.
Underline the things that give direction.

UNDERSTAND

Let's apply the reading skills you covered in Units 1–5.

Camping Safety

People like to go camping. They camp in parks. Sometimes they camp in the woods. But they must be careful! Wild animals live in these areas! One animal to watch out for is the bear.

Bears sleep all winter long. When they wake up, they are very hungry. They go on a search for food. Hungry bears smell food from campers. A hungry bear can smell food from far away. They have big noses with thousands of smell **receptors**. Bears can smell better than people. A bear's sense of smell is even better than that of hunting dogs. Some **scientists** think it is the best of any land animal.

Campers can stay safe by keeping their campsite clean. Left-over food should be stored. Other food that is trash should be put in trashcans. Some parks have garbage cans with locks. The bears cannot get into the locked cans.

Bears move around quietly. They do not make much noise. If a camper happens to meet a bear, he or she should make as much noise as possible. This may scare the bear. If a bear is scared, it will make loud grunting or blowing noises and run away.

Campers can have fun as long as they watch out for bears and follow safety rules.

Units 1–5 Stop and Think! Understand

> **glossary**
> **Scientist:** A person who is trained in science.
> **Receptor:** A sense organ.

Use "Camping Safety" to answer the following questions.

1. What causes a bear to come to a campsite?

    A. Making a lot of noise
    B. Leaving food around
    C. Putting garbage in metal cans

2. What do bears do when they wake up?

    A. They hunt for food.
    B. They go swimming.
    C. They make grunting noises.

3. What is the passage **mostly about**?

    A. Bear's senses
    B. Camping safety
    C. Wild animals

4. Which **key detail** supports the main idea?

    A. People like to go camping.
    B. Bears sleep all winter long.
    C. Campers can stay safe by keeping their campsite clean.

Stop and Think! Understand — Units 1–5

5. What causes a bear to make loud, blowing noises?

   A. It is angry.

   B. It is hungry.

   C. It is scared.

6. What is true about bears?

   A. Bears can open locked cans.

   B. Bears have very small noses.

   C. Bears have a good sense of smell.

Ming Lee's Camping Checklist

Camping is a lot of fun. It is also hard work. Here is a checklist of things to do before a camping trip.

1. Invite family and friends.
2. Pack the tent, matches, lantern, cooler, drinks, food, cooking utensils, sleeping bags, and fishing poles.
3. Pack the first aid kit.
4. Drive to the campground and get a camping spot.

Janesha's Camping Checklist
- Tent
- Sleeping bags
- Sunscreen
- Bug spray
- Bandages
- Hand soap
- Emergency blanket
- Safety whistle
- Compass
- Rain coats
- Matches
- Lantern
- Rope

Units 1–5 Stop and Think! Understand

Ming Lee and Janesha's families are going on a camping trip. Help them prepare for the trip by answering the following questions.

1. How are the two checklists the same?

    A. They both talk about things to take camping.

    B. They both talk about inviting friends and family.

    C. They both talk about finding a good camping spot.

2. How are the checklists different?

    A. Ming Lee's checklist has first aid items and Janesha's does not.

    B. Ming Lee's checklist has sleeping equipment and Janesha's does not.

    C. Ming Lee's checklist has food items and Janesha's does not.

3. Which item is in Ming Lee's checklist that is not in Janesha's checklist?

    A. Sleeping bags

    B. Lantern

    C. Fishing poles

4. Which item is in Janesha's checklist that is not in Ming Lee's checklist?

    A. Rope   B. Tent   C. Matches

DISCOVER

What would you say? Take what you have learned and write about it!

Write a story about going on a trip somewhere. Describe what it is like on your trip.

1. What is your event?

2. Describe what happened in the order in which the events occurred.

3. How did you react to the event?

Draw a picture to illustrate your story.

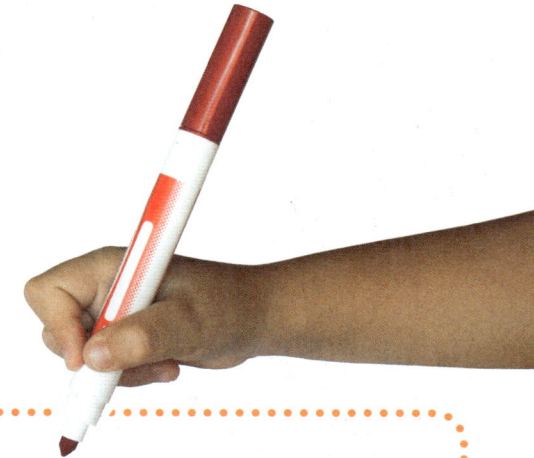

Reading and Writing: Literature

Reading and Writing: Literature

Listen as your adult helper reads the stories aloud. Then, try reading a few sentences yourself.

Remember to use the following reading strategies:

- Read the title and think of the story
- Look at the picture clues
- Start the word—say the beginning sounds
- Look for familiar parts in a word
- Reread to improve understanding and/or to improve fluency
- Read ahead and use the words after to help you figure out the unknown word

Nursery Rhymes and Poetry

UNIT 6

Poetry is a special kind of writing. A single piece of poetry is called a poem. With help from an adult you will practice reading and writing poetry.

Mary's Lamb

Mary had a little lamb,
    Its fleece was white as snow,
And everywhere that Mary went
    The lamb was sure to go;
He followed her to school one day—
    That was against the rule,
It made the children laugh and play,
    To see a lamb at school.

Reading and Writing: Literature

UNDERSTANDING THE KEY DETAILS

Use "Mary's Lamb" to answer the following questions.

1. What color is Mary's lamb?
   A. Black   B. Brown   C. White

2. What was against the rule at Mary's school?
   A. A child having a lamb
   B. A lamb being at school
   C. A child playing at school

3. What did the children do when they saw the lamb?
   A. cry   B. run   C. laugh

4. Use the pictures to retell the story.

Unit 6: Nursery Rhymes and Poetry

ASK QUESTIONS ABOUT UNKNOWN WORDS

1. Read this sentence from "Mary's Lamb."

   "Its **fleece** was white as snow,"

   Which word has the same long "e" vowel sound as the word fleece?

   A. me   B. tent   C. jet

2. **Fleece** is a sheep's wooly coat. Circle the picture that shows a sheep's fleece.

   A.

   B.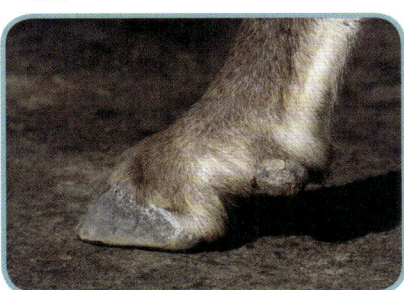

   C.

Digging Deeper

Help Mary and her lamb get to school!
For this activity you will need a separate sheet of paper and your favorite crayons or coloring pencils. Draw a picture of the path that Mary and the lamb must take to get to school. Are there any hills they may have to climb? Do they go through a forest? Do they go through city streets? Do they stop at stop signs? Are there many houses along the way? Do they have to watch out for cars to be safe? Draw your picture! Then share it with your family.

Reading and Writing: Literature

RECOGNIZING POEMS

A **poem** can tell a story. It can describe or tell more about something. A poem often rhymes. When something rhymes, it has rhythm, like a song.

Read the poem. Follow the pattern. Fill in the missing lines.

My Senses

I hear sounds here and there
I hear sounds everywhere
Loud and quiet, low and high
I hear a jet up in the sky!

I see colors here and there
I see colors everywhere
Colors blue and colors red
_____

I taste something here and there
I taste something everywhere
Salty, spicy, sour, and sweet
_____

Unit 6: Nursery Rhymes and Poetry

PRACTICE WRITING UPPER- AND LOWERCASE LETTERS

Say the name of each picture. Write the first letter of each picture in both uppercase and lowercase letters.

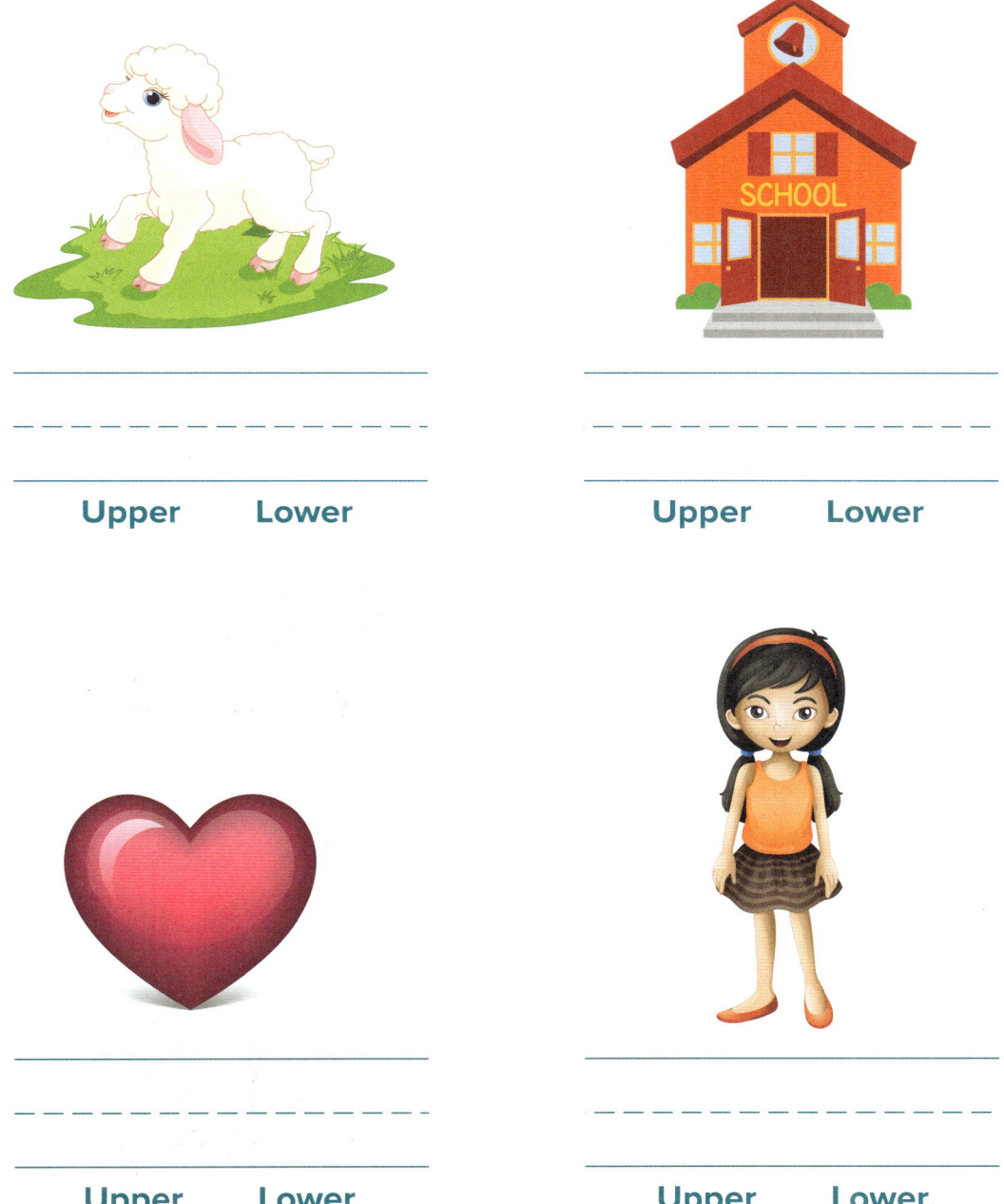

Upper   Lower

Upper   Lower

Upper   Lower

Upper   Lower

Reading and Writing: Literature

SHORT VOWEL SOUNDS

Look at each picture. Fill in the blank with the correct short vowel.

h ___ g

b ___ ll

c ___ p

l ___ g

f ___ sh

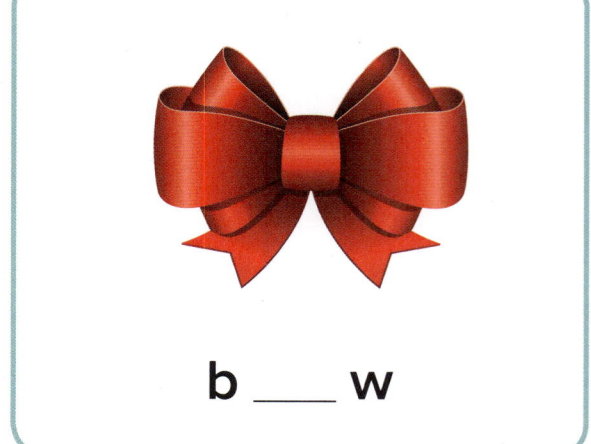

b ___ w

Unit 6: Nursery Rhymes and Poetry

OPPOSITE WORDS

Match the pictures to their opposites. Circle the picture with the opposite meaning.

Reading and Writing: Literature

WRITE YOUR OPINION

Did you like the poem about Mary's lamb? Why or why not? Write and draw your opinion. Use a separate piece of paper if you need more room.

I (liked/did not like) "Mary's Lamb."

I feel this way because:

Conclusion:

Unit 7

Fables

Some stories are told just for fun. Other stories teach lessons. One type of story that teaches a lesson is called a *fable*. Fables are usually very short stories. They have characters that are animals, but the animals talk and act like people. The moral, or lesson, that the fable is teaching is usually at the end. Sometimes one of the characters says the moral or it is a sentence that follows the story. Other times, you may have to figure out the moral or lesson on your own.

The Ant and the Dove

An ant came down to the river. He wanted to drink. Just then, a wave washed him down the river. He almost **drowned**. Poor ant! He cannot swim.

A flying dove carried a branch. She could see that the ant needed help. She threw the branch to him. The ant got up on the branch and was saved.

When the ant got back on the land, he saw a hunter. Oh no! The hunter was getting ready to throw a heavy stone at the dove. Poor dove! But the ant crawled up to the hunter and bit him on the leg. The hunter screamed and dropped the stone. The dove fluttered upwards and flew away.

Moral: If you help others, others will help you in return.

Digging Deeper

Egg Carton Ants

For a fun arts and craft activity, create your own ant! Visit the following website: www.dltk-kids.com/crafts/insects/mant.htm

Make sure you have an empty egg carton so that you can do the activity! Ask an adult or friend to help you complete the project.

Unit 7: Fables

MAIN CHARACTERS, SETTINGS, AND EVENTS

Use "The Ant and the Dove" to answer the following questions.

1. Who are the main **characters**?

   _____

2. Where is the **setting** of the story?

   A. near a tree
   B. at the river
   C. in the sky

3. What is one problem in the story?

   A. The hunter is bitten.
   B. The ant is drowning.
   C. The dove has a branch.

4. How did the ant save the dove?

   A. He threw a branch.
   B. He bit the hunter's leg.
   C. He threw a rock at the hunter.

5. What is the **moral** of this story?

   _____
   _____
   _____

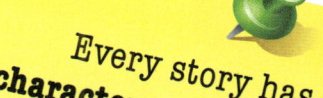

Every story has **main characters**, or who the story is mostly about. Stories also take place in a particular location, which is called the **setting**. A setting can be anywhere the author chooses—a park, the ocean, a school, or a lake.

The **moral** of the story is the lesson that it teaches.

Standard RL.K.1, RL.K.3

Reading and Writing: Literature

PICTURES HELP YOU UNDERSTAND THE STORY

1. What moment in the story does this image show?

    A. An ant came down to the river.

    B. The dove will help the ant by giving him a branch.

    C. The ant crawled up on the branch and was saved.

2. What is happening in the picture below?

    A. The ant was getting ready to swim.

    B. The ant crawled up on the hunter and bit him on the leg.

    C. The hunter was getting ready to throw a stone at the dove.

Unit 7: Fables

ASK QUESTIONS ABOUT UNKNOWN WORDS

Adults: Help your student answer the activity questions on this page by using picture clues and other word clues from the story. You can also ask the prompt questions for each.

Activity 1

Read these two sentences from the story.

"A wave washed him down the river. He almost **drowned**."

What does the word **drowned** mean?

Think . . . the first sentence is a clue. It says, a wave washed him down the river. What do you know about washing?

When you wash something, you use a lot of water. So in this sentence, the word **drowned** means that the ant was:

A. sitting on top of the water

B. covered with water

C. swimming in the water

word bank: flutter, river, stone

Activity 2

Fill in the sentences with the correct word from the word bank.

1. The log floated down the _____.
   Ask: What is a stream of water called?

2. The boy threw a _____ at the giant.
   Ask: What is light enough for a boy to pick up and throw?

3. The book pages _____ in the wind.
   Ask: What does the wind do to things?

Standard RL.K.4

Reading and Writing: Literature

RECOGNIZE COMPLETE AND INCOMPLETE SENTENCES

A sentence is a group of words that makes a complete thought. It begins with a capital letter and ends with an end mark. A sentence will have **a subject** and **a predicate**. The subject tells who or what the sentence is about. The predicate will express what is said about the subject.

Examples:

Complete:
The dove has strong wings.
The ant is a busy worker.
The hunter watched the birds.

Incomplete:
The dove has strong.
The ant worker.
Watched the birds.

Underline the complete sentences. Put a line through the incomplete sentences.

1. Hunter the dove.

2. The is white.

3. Ants can make anthills.

4. Is read stories.

5. She stops to pick flowers.

Unit 7: Fables

USING END PUNCTUATION

Underline the correct end punctuation for each sentence. (! ? .)

1. I saw a dove ! ? .
2. Where is the ant ! ? .
3. Don't fall in the river ! ? .
4. Watch out for the bears ! ? .
5. Why would anyone hurt a bird ! ? .
6. The ant and dove are friends ! ? .
7. My dad fishes in the river ! ? .

USING CAPITAL LETTERS

A sentence always begins with a capital letter.

> Examples: The boy is a shepherd.
>
> The pronoun **I** is always capitalized even when it is in the middle of a sentence.
>
> When I see a funny movie I laugh.

Capitalize the correct words in each sentence below.

1. riding the bus to school is fun.
2. you and i can go to the store.
3. on sunny days i go to the beach.
4. we can have fun at the park.
5. i like to go camping at the lake.

Standards L.K.2.a, L.K.2.b

Reading and Writing: Literature

UNDERSTANDING QUESTION WORDS

You ask questions to find out information. Special words are used to show that you are asking a question.

What do these special words mean?

Who = asks about people.
> Who is your best friend?

Where = asks for a location.
> Where is your notebook?

When = asks for a time or occasion.
> When will you take your vacation?

Why = asks for an explanation or a reason.
> Why do you like to read?

Which = asks for a choice to be made.
> Which book will you choose to read?

How = asks about the way something will be done.
> How will you complete your project?

Unit 7: Fables

Using the word bank, fill in the sentences with the correct question word.

word bank: Who   Where   What   Why   Which   How

1. _____ does the ant go?
2. _____ is going to throw a stone?
3. _____ was the man going to throw?
4. _____ did the dove know the ant was drowning?
5. _____ did the ant want to help the dove?
6. _____ character almost drowned?

BECOME A GOOD SPELLER

You can use letter sounds to help you spell words.

Look at the picture. Say the word. What sound do you hear at the beginning of the word?

Now, sound out the rest of the word, and write those letter sounds too!

_____   _____   _____

Standard L.K.2.a

Reading and Writing: Literature

Complete each sentence by correctly spelling the word that is shown in the picture.

1. The _____ was shining over the river.

2. I saw a _____ on the lake.

3. A man caught a _____.

4. The man put the _____ into the water.

5. It got dark and the _____ came out.

6. The _____ twinkled in the night sky.

Unit 7: Fables

REAL-LIFE CONNECTIONS

Activity 1

Look at the words on the left. These are adjectives, or words that describe nouns. Draw a line to match the adjectives to the nouns on the right. Remember, a noun is a person, place, or thing.

adjective	noun
slimy	flowers
cold	ice cream
bright	sun
colorful	worm

Activity 2

Now that you have matched up your adjectives and nouns, use these word pairs to complete each sentence below. Think about where you would see or use these things in real life.

1. I see a _____ in the dirt at the park.

2. I like to eat _____ on a hot sunny.

3. I wear sunglasses when I am out in the _____ .

4. I see many _____ in my grandmother's garden.

Standard L.K.5.c

Reading and Writing: Literature

SHADES OF MEANING

If you want to color a picture of a pretty blue sky on a sunny day, which color blue will you choose from your box of crayons? It would be important to choose the right color blue. You would not choose a dark blue crayon; if you did then it would be nighttime! Just like choosing the right color is important for your picture, it is important to choose the right words for what you want to say.

Adults: Have students act out the following action verbs.

1. rinse, wash, scrub
2. eat, gobble, nibble
3. talk, whisper, mutter
4. stroll, tiptoe, stride

> Some words have almost the same meaning. Understanding the differences between similar words can help you describe things more clearly.

REVIEW

Congratulations! You have completed the lessons in Units 6–7. Now you will have the opportunity to practice some of the skills you just learned.

The Boy Who Cried Wolf

A boy was watching a flock of sheep. He wanted to play a trick on the farmers.

So he pretended that he saw a wolf. He cried, "Help! A wolf! A wolf!" The farmers came running up. But there was no wolf. The boy was telling a lie.

The boy thought it was funny. So again he cried, "Help! A wolf! A wolf!" The farmers left their dinner and came running. But again, there was not a wolf anywhere. The farmers went home.

Later on, a wolf really did come. The boy was so scared! He cried as loud as he could, "Help! A wolf! A wolf!" But the farmers did not come this time. They thought the boy was tricking them again. The wolf was not afraid of the boy. The wolf ran off with two of the sheep. And the boy never told a lie again.

Moral: If you lie people will not believe you when you tell the truth.

Digging Deeper

Adults, make stick puppets or headbands and have students retell the story. Teach students the importance of responsibility and honesty. Have students role play for reinforcement.

Units 6–7 Stop and Think! Review

Activity 1

Fill in the sentences with the correct question word (*Who, What, Where, When, Why,* or *How*).

1. _____ many times did the boy cry wolf?

2. _____ did the boy lie?

3. _____ happened to the sheep?

4. _____ were the farmers when the wolf came?

Activity 2

Underline the complete sentences and place the correct end punctuation. Circle the words that should be capitalized. Write those words properly on the lines below.

i like _____

The wolf is mean _____

the sheep are sleeping _____

The boy yelled _____

when are they coming home _____

Help, i see a wolf _____

Stop and Think! Review   Units 6–7

Activity 3

Place the correct end punctuation in the sentences below.

1. Look out for the wolf
2. Please don't tell a lie
3. How many sheep are in the field
4. Oh no, the sheep are gone

Activity 4

Place the correct letters in the boxes to spell the picture word.

Activity 5

Adults: Have students act out the following action verbs.

1. jump, hop, bounce
2. walk, march, strut
3. look, stare, glare
4. toss, throw, pitch
5. run, jog, sprint

UNDERSTAND

Let's apply the reading skills you covered in Units 6–7.

Little Red Riding Hood

Once upon a time there lived a pretty little girl. She always wore the red cape and hood that her grandmother made for her. So everyone called her Little Red Riding Hood. One day her mother asked her if she would take her grandmother a basket of treats. Little Red Riding Hood set out to her grandmother's house. On her way she met a mean, hungry wolf.

"Where are you going?" asked the wolf.

"I'm going to see my grandmother. She lives in a house behind those trees." said Little Red Riding Hood. The wolf ran as fast as he could to grandmother's house. He locked her in a closet. Little Red Riding Hood was busy picking flowers in the wood. The wolf got into grandmother's bed. He pulled the covers up and waited. A little later, Little Red Riding Hood reached the house. She looked at the wolf.

"Grandma, what big eyes you have!"

"The better to see you with!" said the wolf.

"Grandma, what big ears you have!"

"The better to hear you with!" said the wolf.

"Grandma, what a big nose you have!"
"The better to smell you with!" said the wolf.
"But, grandma what big teeth you have!"
"The better to eat you with!" shouted the wolf.

A hunter was in the wood. He heard a loud scream and ran to the house. The hunter hit the wolf over the head. Little Red Riding Hood let her grandmother out of the closet. The wolf ran away and Little Red Riding Hood never saw him again!

Moral: Don't talk to strangers!

Activity 1

Use "Little Red Riding Hood" to answer the following questions.

1. Why did everyone call the girl Little Red Riding Hood?
    A. She had red hair.
    B. She liked the color red.
    C. She always wore a red cape.

2. Where does the last part of the story take place?
    A. in the woods
    B. at grandma's house
    C. at Little Red Riding Hood's house

3. What is the main problem in the story?

_____

Units 6–7   Stop and Think! Understand

4. Which character solved the problem?

   A. The hunter   B. The wolf   C. The girl

5. Place the number in the boxes below each picture in the order in which they happened.

6. A storybook has a beginning, a _____, and an end.

7. Which person draws the pictures in a book?

   A. author   B. illustrator   C. publisher

8. What does the author do?

   A. writes the story

   B. draws the pictures

   C. sells the book

Stop and Think! Understand 6–7

Activity 2

Compare and contrast "Mary's Lamb" and "Little Red Riding Hood" by filling out the Venn diagram.

Mary's Lamb (different)

Same

Little Red Riding Hood (different)

Standard RL.K.9

Units 6–7 Stop and Think! Understand

Activity 3

The paragraph below has six made-up words in it. Replace the silly words with words from the bank below. Use the clues around the made-up words to help you figure out what the correct word should be.

A girl went for a kure in the woods. For as far as her lak could see were colorful flowers. She stopped to pick the beautiful jluo. She heard a scary oiehi and turned around. Standing behind her was a zzue wolf. She blel back home as fast as she could go.

1. _____
2. _____
3. _____
4. _____
5. _____
6. _____

word bank

ran
noise
eyes
flowers
hungry
walk

Digging Deeper

Don't Talk to Strangers!
Have students role play what to do and say if a stranger approaches them. Keep kids safe by visiting the link for stranger-danger songs, activities, and games. www.free-for-kids.com/stranger-danger.shtml

DISCOVER

Understand the meaning of what you have learned and apply your knowledge.

Share Your Opinion

Which story did you like the most—"The Ant and the Dove," "The Boy Who Cried Wolf," or "Little Red Riding Hood?" Write and draw your opinion. Use a separate piece of paper if you need more room.

My opinion is:

_____

_____

_____

Standard W.K.1

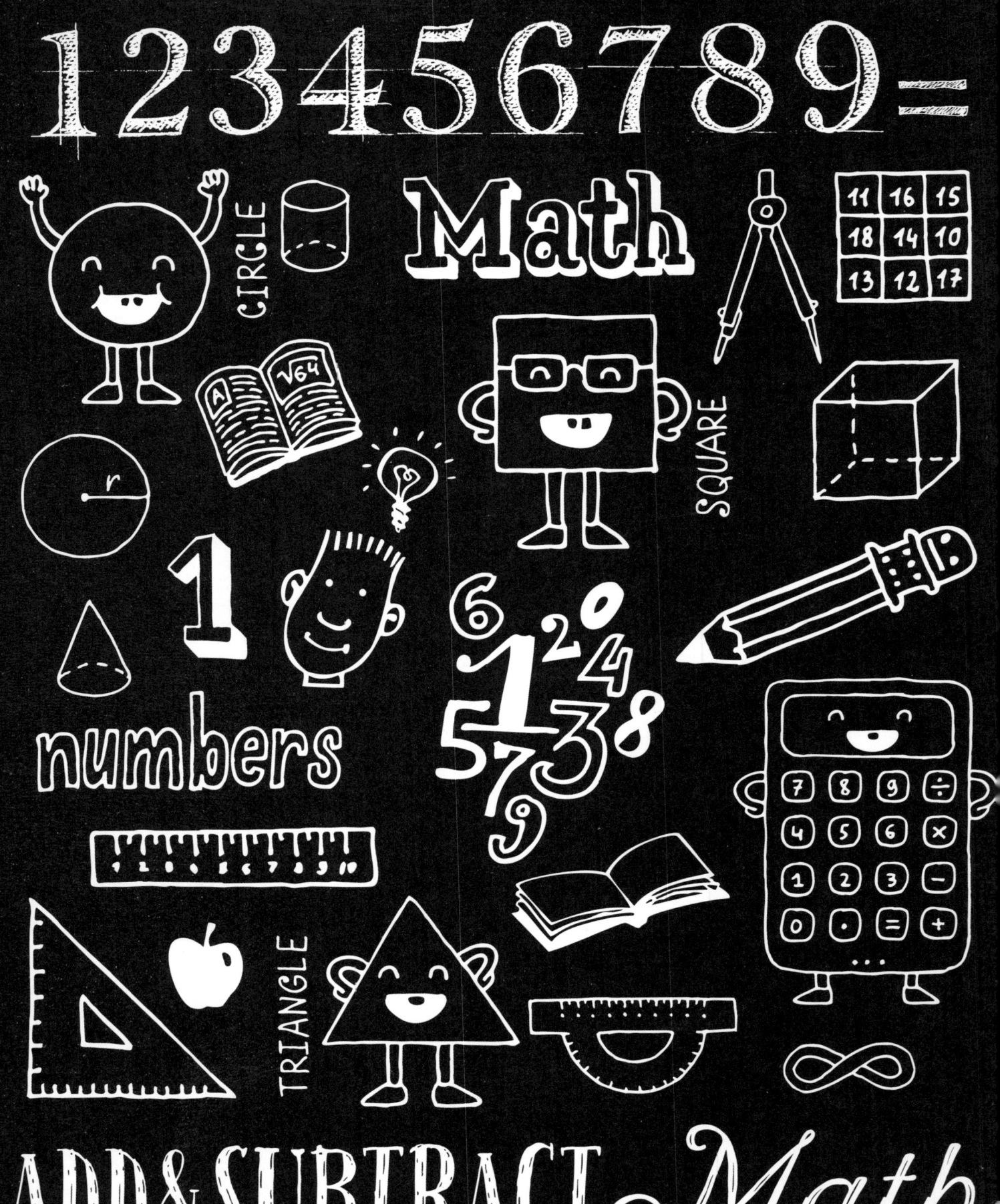

Math

Introduction to Problem-Solving and Mathematical Practices

Geometry

Identifying and Describing Two-Dimensional Shapes

CCSS.MATH,CONTENT.K.G.A.1 – Describe objects in the environment using names of shapes, and describe the relative positions of these objects using terms such as *above, below, beside, in front of, behind,* and *next to.*

CCSS.MATH,CONTENT.K.G.A.2 – Correctly name shapes regardless of their orientations or overall size.

CCSS.MATH,CONTENT.K.G.A.3 – Identify shapes as two-dimensional (lying in a plane, "flat") or three-dimensional ("solid").

CCSS.MATH,CONTENT.K.G.B.4 – Analyze and compare two- and three-dimensional shapes, in different sizes and orientations, using informal language to describe their similarities, differences, parts (e.g., number of sides and vertices/"corners") and other attributes (e.g., having sides of equal length).

CCSS.MATH,CONTENT.K.G.B.5 – Model shapes in the world by building shapes from components (e.g., sticks and clay balls) and drawing shapes.

CCSS.MATH,CONTENT.K.G.B.6 – Compose simple shapes to form larger shapes. For example, *"Can you join these two triangles with full sides touching to make a rectangle?"*

Counting and Cardinality

Counting, Comparing, and Writing Numbers 0–10.

CCSS.MATH,CONTENT.K.CC.A.1 – Count to 100 by ones and by tens.

CCSS.MATH,CONTENT.K.CC.A.2 – Count forward beginning from a given number within the known sequence (instead of having to begin at 1).

CCSS.MATH,CONTENT.K.CC.A.3 – Write numbers from 0–20. Represent a number of objects with a written numeral 0–20 (with 0 representing a count of no objects). NOTE: This standard will be repeated throughout the year.

CCSS.MATH,CONTENT.K.CC.B.4 – Understand the relationships between numbers and quantities; connect counting to cardinality.

CCSS.MATH,CONTENT.K.CC.B.4A – When counting objects, say the number names in the standard order, pairing each object with one and only one number name and each number name with one and only one object.

CCSS.MATH,CONTENT.K.CC.B.4B – Understand that the last number name said tells the number of objects counted. The number of objects is the same regardless of their arrangement or the order in which they were counted.

CCSS.MATH,CONTENT.K.CC.B.4C – Understand that each successive number name refers to a quantity that is one larger.

CCSS.MATH,CONTENT.K.CC.B.5 – Count to answer "how many?" questions about as many as 20 things arranged in a line, a rectangular array, or a circle, or as many as 10 things in a scattered configuration; given a number from 1–20, count out that many objects.

CCSS.MATH,CONTENT.K.CC.C.6 – Identify whether the number of objects in one group is greater than, less than, or equal to the number of objects in another group, e.g., by using matching and counting strategies.

CCSS.MATH,CONTENT.K.CC.C.7 – Compare two numbers between 1 and 10 presented as written numerals.

Measurement and Data

Measuring

CCSS.MATH,CONTENT.K.MD.A.1 – Describe measurable attributes of objects, such as length or weight. Describe several measurable attributes of a single object.

CCSS.MATH,CONTENT.K.MD.A.2 – Directly compare two objects with a measurable attribute in common to see which object has "more of"/"less of" the attribute, and describe the difference. For example, directly compare the heights of two children and describe one child as taller/shorter.

CCSS.MATH,CONTENT.K.MD.B.3 – Classify objects into a given categories; count the numbers of objects in each category and sort the categories by count (category counts to be less than or equal to 10).

Classifying and Sorting Data

CCSS.MATH,CONTENT.3.MD.B.3 – Classify objects into given categories; count the numbers of objects in each category and sort the categories by count.

Counting and Cardinality and Number Operations in Base-Ten

Working with Numbers 11–19

CCSS.MATH,CONTENT.K.NBT.A.1 – Compose and decompose numbers from 11 to 19 into ten ones and some further ones, e.g., by using objects or drawings,

Introduction to Problem-Solving and Mathematical Practices

and record each composition or decomposition by drawing or equation (e.g., 18 = 10 + 8); understand that these numbers are composed of ten ones and one, two, three, four, five, six, seven, eight, or nine ones.

CCSS.MATH,CONTENT.K.CC.A.1 – Count to 100 by ones and by tens.

CCSS.MATH,CONTENT.K.CC.A.2 – Count forward beginning from a given number within the known sequence (instead of having to begin at 1).

CCSS.MATH,CONTENT.K.CC.A.3 – Write numbers from 0–20. Represent a number of objects with a written numeral 0–20 (with 0 representing a count of no objects). NOTE: This standard will be repeated throughout the year.

CCSS.MATH,CONTENT.K.CC.B.4 – Understand the relationships between numbers and quantities; connect counting to cardinality.

CCSS.MATH,CONTENT.K.CC.B.4A – When counting objects, say the number names in the standard order, pairing each object with one and only one number name and each number name with one and only one object.

CCSS.MATH,CONTENT.K.CC.B.4B – Understand that the last number name said tells the number of objects counted. The number of objects is the same regardless of their arrangement or the order in which they were counted.

CCSS.MATH,CONTENT.K.CC.B.4C – Understand that each successive number name refers to a quantity that is one larger.

CCSS.MATH,CONTENT.K.CC.B.5 – Count to answer "how many?" questions about as many as 20 things arranged in a line, a rectangular array, or a circle, or as many as 10 things in a scattered configuration; given a number from 1–20, count out that many objects.

CCSS.MATH,CONTENT.K.CC.C.6 – Identify whether the number of objects in one group is greater than, less than, or equal to the number of objects in another group, e.g., by using matching and counting strategies.

CCSS.MATH,CONTENT.K.CC.C.7 – Compare two numbers between 1 and 10 presented as written numerals.

Operations and Algebraic Thinking

Adding

CCSS.MATH,CONTENT.K.OA.A.1 – Represent addition and subtraction with objects, fingers, mental images drawings, sounds (e.g., claps), acting out situations, verbal explanations, expressions, or equations.

CCSS.MATH,CONTENT.K.OA.A.2 – Solve addition and subtraction word problems, and add and subtract within 10, e.g., by using objects or drawings, to represent the problem.

CCSS.MATH,CONTENT.K.OA.A.3 – Decompose numbers less than or equal to 10 into pairs in more than one way, e.g., by using objects or drawings, and record each decomposition by drawing or equation (e.g., 5 = 2 + 3 and 5 = 4 + 1).

CCSS.MATH,CONTENT.K.OA.A.4 – For any number from 1 to 9, find the number that makes 10 when added to the given number, e.g., by using objects or drawings, and record the answer with a drawing or equation.

CCSS.MATH,CONTENT.K.OA.A.5 – Fluently add and subtract within 5.

Subtracting

CCSS.MATH,CONTENT.K.OA.A.1 – Represent addition and subtraction with objects, fingers, mental images drawings, sounds (e.g., claps), acting out situations, verbal explanations, expressions, or equations.

CCSS.MATH,CONTENT.K.OA.A.2 – Solve addition and subtraction word problems, and add and subtract within 10, e.g., by using objects or drawings, to represent the problem.

CCSS.MATH,CONTENT.K.OA.A.5 – Fluently add and subtract within 5.

Counting and Cardinality

Counting and Writing Numbers to 20 and Beyond

CCSS.MATH,CONTENT.K.CC.A.1 – Count to 100 by ones and by tens.

CCSS.MATH,CONTENT.K.CC.A.2 – Count forward beginning from a given number within the known sequence (instead of having to begin at 1).

CCSS.MATH,CONTENT.K.CC.A.3 – Write numbers from 0–20. Represent a number of objects with a written numeral 0–20 (with 0 representing a count of no objects). NOTE: This standard will be repeated throughout the year.

CCSS.MATH,CONTENT.K.CC.B.4 – Understand the relationships between numbers and quantities; connect counting to cardinality.

CCSS.MATH,CONTENT.K.CC.B.4A – When counting objects, say the number names in the standard order, pairing each object with one and only one number name and each number name with one and only one object.

CCSS.MATH,CONTENT.K.CC.B.4B – Understand that the last number name said tells the number of objects counted. The number of objects is the same regardless of their arrangement or the order in which they were counted.

CCSS.MATH,CONTENT.K.CC.B.4C – Understand that each successive number name refers to a quantity that is one larger.

CCSS.MATH,CONTENT.K.CC.B.5 – Count to answer "how many?" questions about as many as 20 things arranged in a line, a rectangular array, or a circle, or as many as 10 things in a scattered configuration; given a number from 1–20, count out that many objects.

CCSS.MATH,CONTENT.K.CC.C.6 – Identify whether the number of objects in one group is greater than, less than, or equal to the number of objects in another group, e.g., by using matching and counting strategies.

CCSS.MATH,CONTENT.K.CC.C.7 – Compare two numbers between 1 and 10 presented as written numerals.

Making Sense of the Problem-Solving Process

This first chapter will address the problem-solving process aligned to the checklist in the **Ace It Time!** section of each lesson. Ace It Time! will help your student master the eight mathematical practices. Each of the eight mathematical practices address the rigor and complexity of problem-solving that Common Core demands. Students and parents must have strategies to solve these problems successfully. Problem solving in the mathematics classroom is no longer just about computation alone; it encompasses a student's ability to persevere, reason, justify, model, and explain.

While Doing Mathematics, Kindergarten Grade Students Will . . .

1. Make sense of problems and become a champion in solving them

- Solve problems and have discussions about how they solved them
- Make sense (meaning) of a problem and search for a solution
- Look for a starting point and have a plan to solve their problems
- Use what they already know about a concept to help them solve their problems
- Use concrete objects or pictures to help them understand and find solutions for the problem
- Check their work by asking themselves questions (i.e., "Does this make sense?")
- Be willing to listen to the strategies of their peers and be willing to try various approaches to solve problems and check their work

2. Reason abstractly and quantitatively

- Understand that numbers represent exact quantities
- Connect quantities to written symbols
- Be able to (decontextualize) take a word problem and represent it with numbers and symbols and (contextualize) make sense out of the numbers and symbols in a problem

3. Construct viable arguments and critique the reasoning of others

- Explain their thinking to others and be able to respond to the thinking of others
- Practice having conversations/discussions about math
- Have math discussions and use objects, pictures, and/or drawings to help them explain or defend their answers
- Ask questions to clarify the thinking of others (i.e., "How did you get that answer? How do you know?")
- Be able to justify their answers and determine if the thinking of others is correct or incorrect

Making Sense of the Problem-Solving Process

4. Model with mathematics
- Use the math they know to solve everyday problems
- Should be able to represent story problems in different ways; examples of these representations are as follows: numbers, words, drawings, pictures, using objects or manipualtives, acting out, making charts, making lists, constructing equations, etc.
- Have opportunities to make connections between these representations and explain
- Are able to evaluate their answers or solutions and reflect on whether or not they make sense

5. Use appropriate tools strategically
- Use available tools when solving math problems (including estimations)
- Be able to choose tools appropriately and determine which tools and when they might be helpful
- Use technology to help with their understanding

6. Attend to detail
- Develop math communication skills by using clear and precise language in their math conversation
- Calculate efficiently and accurately

7. Look for and make use of structure
- Apply general math rules to specific situations
- Look for patterns or structure to help them solve their problems; for example, they might recognize that every teen number is written with a 1, which represents one 10

8. Look for and express regularity in repeated reasoning
- Notice how things repeat in their computation and look for shortcut methods to solve their problems; for example, they might notice that the next number in a counting sequence is one more

For the official Standards of Mathematical Practice, please visit www.corestandards.org

UNIT 1: CORE Problem-Solving Concepts

UNPACK THE STANDARD
You will learn how to solve word problems.

LEARN IT: You are going to learn how to solve different math problems. You will learn more about numbers, shapes, and measuring. There are steps you can use to solve all kinds of problems. You will use these steps in the *Ace It Time!* part of each lesson.

Step 1: Understand—What's the Question?

- The checklist shows steps you can use to solve a math problem.
- The first step is to read the problem. Ask, "What is the question?"
- Find the question. Trace it with your finger as you read it. Then check "Yes" on the checklist.

PRACTICE: Find the question. Trace it with your finger.

Example: Jacob has 4 balloons. Katie has 6 balloons. <u>Who has more?</u>

Did you find the question?		yes	no
Did you circle helpful numbers and words?	②　How many more? ⓘn all	yes	no
Did you use pictures, counters, or numbers to help you solve?	2 apples	yes	no
Can you explain your thinking in words?		yes	no

CCSS.Math.Content.K.CC.C.7

Unit 1: CORE Problem-Solving Concepts

Step 2: Identify—What Numbers or Words Are Needed?

Find the numbers and words you will use to solve the problem. Circle them. Then check "Yes" on the checklist.

PRACTICE: Circle the numbers and words you need to solve the problem.

Example: Jacob has ④ balloons. Katie has ⑥ balloons. <u>Who has more</u>?

Circle the 4 and 6. Those are the numbers of balloons. Circle the word "more." This word is a clue. It tells us this question is asking us which number is greater! You will compare 4 and 6 to see which is more.

		yes	no
Did you find the question?	How many more?	○	○
Did you circle helpful numbers and words?	②　in all	○	○
Did you use pictures, counters, or numbers to help you solve?	2 apples	○	○
Can you explain your thinking in words?		○	○

Unit 1: CORE Problem-Solving Concepts

Step 3: Use a Model to Solve

You can make a model to help you solve a problem. You can draw a picture to show the problem. You can use counters or other math tools to act out the problem. You can write a number sentence. Choose a good way to model the problem. Then check "Yes" on the checklist.

PRACTICE: Draw a picture to model the problem. Label the picture to help you.

Jacob's balloons — 4

Katie's balloons — 6

Katie has more balloons than Jacob because 6 is greater than 4.

Did you find the question?	*How many more?*	yes no
Did you circle helpful numbers and words?	② in all	yes no
Did you use pictures, counters, or numbers to help you solve?	🍎🍎 2 apples	yes no
Can you explain your thinking in words?	✏️	yes no

104 CCSS.Math.Content.K.CC.C.7

Unit 1: CORE Problem-Solving Concepts

Step 4: Explain Your Thinking

You are almost done! Explain how you got your answer. Tell your adult helper how you solved this problem. You can challenge yourself to write your explanation in words too! The vocabulary words in the blue box below can help you with your explanation.

Example: Jacob has ④ balloons. Katie has ⑥ balloons. Who has more?

"I counted the balloons. 6 is greater than 4. Katie has more balloons than Jacob."

Math Vocabulary

more

greater than

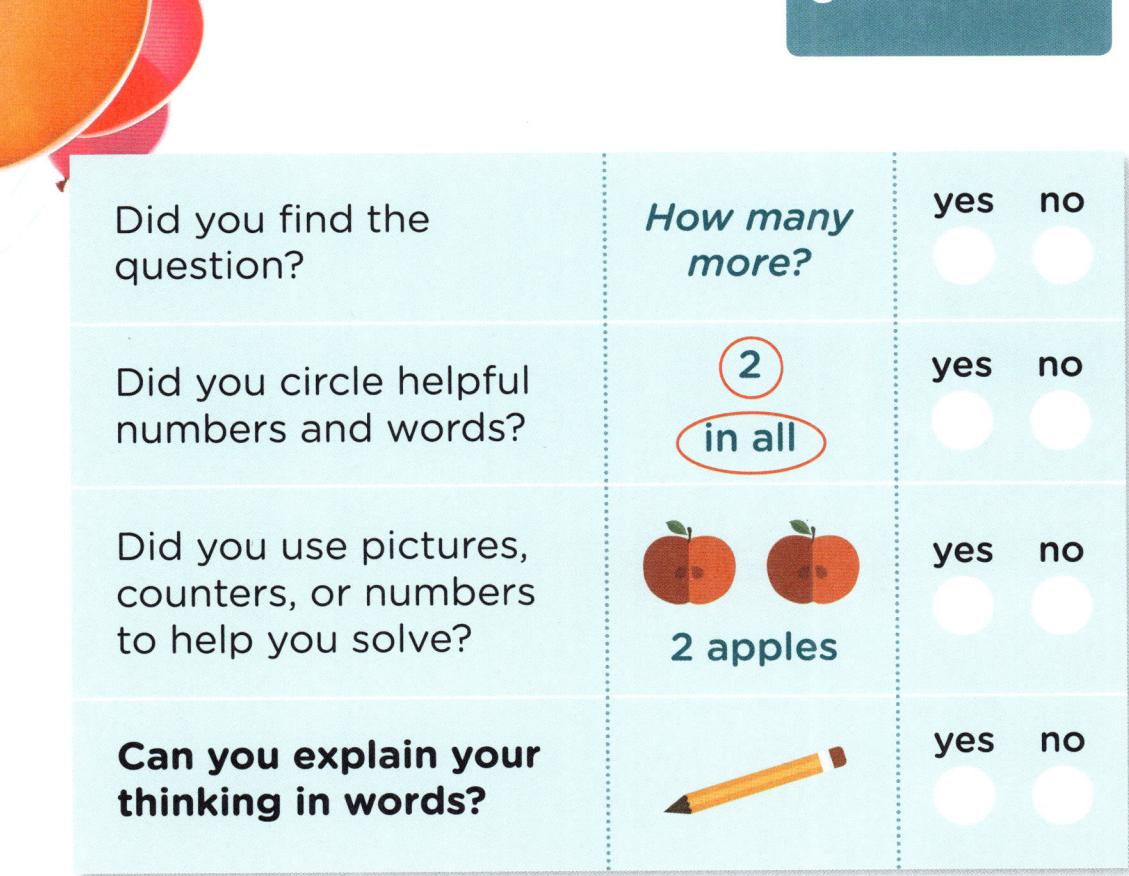

Did you find the question?	*How many more?*	yes no
Did you circle helpful numbers and words?	② in all	yes no
Did you use pictures, counters, or numbers to help you solve?	2 apples	yes no
Can you explain your thinking in words?		yes no

CCSS.Math.Content.K.CC.C.7

UNIT 2

CORE Counting and Number Concepts (Numbers 0–10)

Explore Numbers 1–10

UNPACK THE STANDARD
You will count to numbers up to 10.

LEARN IT: You can count objects in a group. Each number has a name.

Example: Count the objects below.

ruler	1	one
2 lunchboxes	2	two
3 glue bottles	3	three
4 pencils	4	four
5 notebooks	5	five
6 paintbrushes	6	six
7 markers	7	seven
8 crayons	8	eight
9 paperclips	9	nine
10 scissors	10	ten

Explore Numbers 1–10

PRACTICE: Now you try

Count the snap cubes. Write the number.

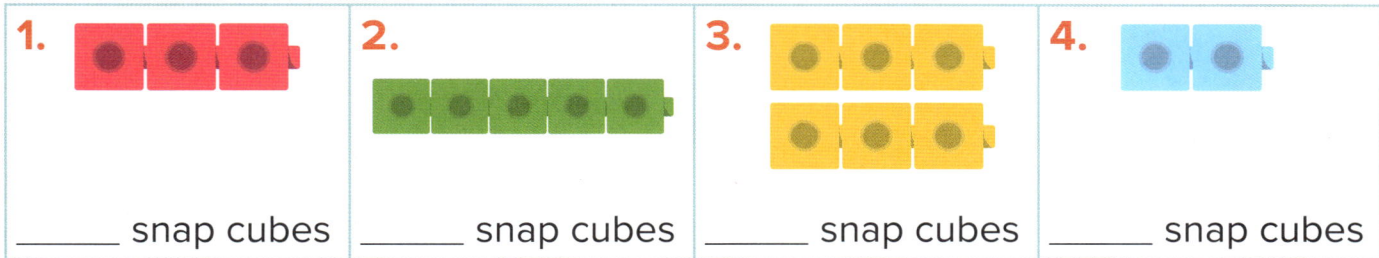

1. _____ snap cubes 2. _____ snap cubes 3. _____ snap cubes 4. _____ snap cubes

Count each set of lunchboxes. Circle the set that shows 7 lunchboxes.

Math Vocabulary

count
number
set
seven
7

Did you find the question?	*How many more?*	yes no
Did you circle helpful numbers and words?	2 in all	yes no
Did you use pictures, counters, or numbers to help you solve?	2 apples	yes no
Can you explain your thinking in words?		yes no

Keep on counting! Look for groups of objects between 1 and 10 around your house. Count the objects and write the number.

CCSS.Math.Content.K.CC.A.1, CC.A.3

Unit 2: CORE Counting and Number Concepts (Numbers 0–10)

Count 0–10

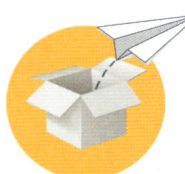

UNPACK THE STANDARD
You will count and write numbers 0 to 10. You will count on from a number.

LEARN IT: You know all the numbers 1 to 10. What about zero? *Zero* is a number that comes before 1. It is written as 0. It means there is nothing in that group!

Example: Kim wants to clean her fish tank. She took all of the fish out of the tank. How many fish are in the tank?

0 fish

You can use what you know about counting from 0 to 10 to count on. Counting on means you say the number that comes next.

Example: Count on from the number 4. Stop at the number 10. Say "4, 5, 6, 7, 8, 9, 10!" Notice how 5 comes after 4. That means 5 is one more than 4!

PRACTICE: Now you try

Count the fish. Write the number.

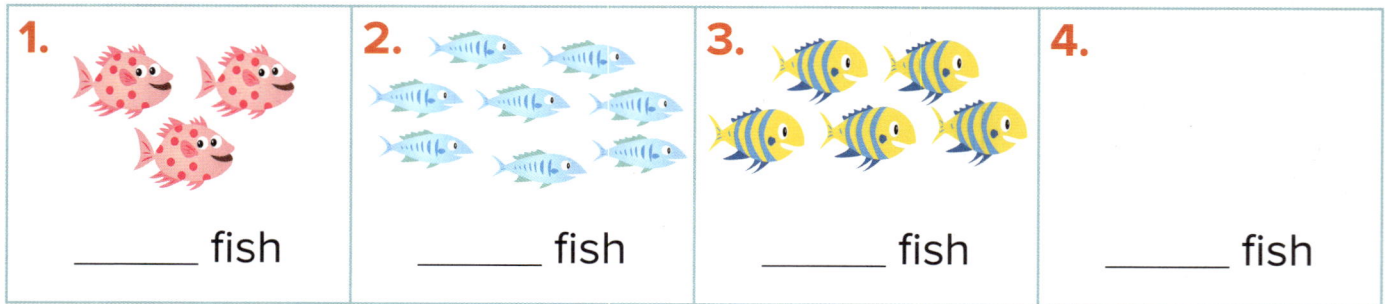

1. _____ fish
2. _____ fish
3. _____ fish
4. _____ fish

Count 0–10

Count on from each number. Write the number on each line. Stop at 10!

5. 6, _____ , _____ , _____ , _____

6. 5, _____ , _____ , _____ , _____ , _____

Count the number of fish in the tank. Touch each fish as you count! Write how many fish are in the tank on the line below. Explain your thinking.

_____

ACE IT TIME!

Math Vocabulary
- count
- count on
- number
- zero

Did you find the question?	*How many more?*	yes no
Did you circle helpful numbers and words?	② (in all)	yes no
Did you use pictures, counters, or numbers to help you solve?	2 apples	yes no
Can you explain your thinking in words?		yes no

MATH ON THE MOVE

Practice counting on! Take turns with a partner. Say a number 0–10. Your partner will count on from that number to 10. Take turns saying numbers and counting on.

Unit 2: CORE Counting and Number Concepts (Numbers 0–10)

How Many?

UNPACK THE STANDARD
You will count to answer "how many."

LEARN IT: You can count numbers in order starting at 0. The numbers get bigger as you count. You can count objects in a group. This tells you *how many* objects are in the group. It does not matter how the objects are grouped. Just remember to touch each object while you count!

Example: Count to find how many there are.

How many stars are there?	How many stars are there?

There are **5** stars.	There are **5** stars.
OR	OR
There are **five** stars.	There are **five** stars.

PRACTICE: Now you try

Count the objects to find how many there are.

1. How many? _____
2. How many? _____
3. How many? _____

How Many?

Count the number of objects in each group. Draw a line to the number that tells how many there are. Explain your thinking.

   4   four

   8   eight

   3   three

ACE IT TIME!

Math Vocabulary

count

number

group

Did you find the question?	*How many more?*	yes no
Did you circle helpful numbers and words?	2 in all	yes no
Did you use pictures, counters, or numbers to help you solve?	2 apples	yes no
Can you explain your thinking in words?		yes no

Practice writing how many there are! Count objects up to 10 around the house. Practice writing the number on paper, in sand, or trace it in the air! Can you write the number very big or super small? You can think of fun ways to count and write how many there are.

CCSS.Math.Content.K.CC.B.4A–K.CC.B.4C, CC.B.5

Unit 2: CORE Counting and Number Concepts (Numbers 0–10)

Greater Than–Less Than–Equal To

UNPACK THE STANDARD
You will tell if a number of objects in one group is greater than, less than, or equal to another group.

LEARN IT: You can use counting or matching to tell if a group is bigger or smaller than another group. Or maybe they are the same size!

Example: Compare the two groups of counters.

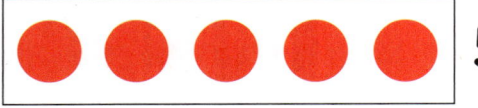 5   Draw lines to match the red counters to the yellow counters.

 3   The top group of counters has more in it. 5 is **greater than** 3.

 2   Draw lines to match the red counters to the yellow counters.

 4   The top group of counters has less in it. 2 is **less than** 4.

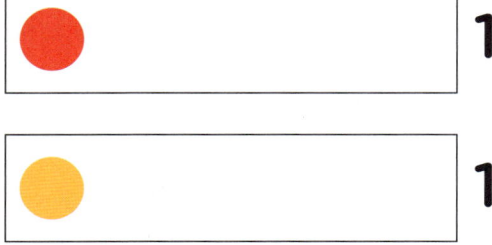

1

1

Draw a line to match the red counter to the yellow counter. Both groups have the same number of counters. They are equal!

Both groups are the same.
1 is **equal to** 1.

Greater Than–Less Than–Equal To

PRACTICE: Now you try

Count the objects. Write the number. Circle the group that has **fewer** objects.

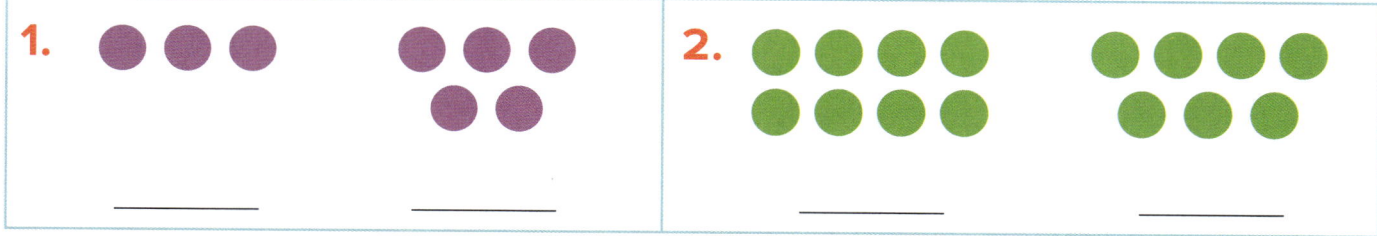

Ally and Shane collected shells on the beach. Count each group. Write the number. Circle the group that is greater. Explain your thinking.

Ally's shells: _____   Shane's shells: _____

Math Vocabulary

greater than

less than

group

equal to

number

Did you find the question?	*How many more?*	yes no
Did you circle helpful numbers and words?	 	yes no
Did you use pictures, counters, or numbers to help you solve?	 2 apples	yes no
Can you explain your thinking in words?		yes no

Look for groups of objects around your house. Which groups are greater? Which groups are less? Can you find any equal groups?

Unit 2: CORE Counting and Number Concepts (Numbers 0–10)

Compare Numbers

UNPACK THE STANDARD
You will compare two numbers between 1 and 10.

LEARN IT: You know how to count from 0 to 10. You know that numbers get bigger as you count. You also know how to tell which group of objects has more than another. Now you can use what you know about numbers 0 through 10 to *compare* them.

Example: Which is greater, 7 or 8?

We can solve this by using what we know about numbers. Think of counting in order. Think "0, 1, 2, 3, 4, 5, 6, 7, 8, 9, 10." We count 7 before 8. That means 8 is bigger, or greater, than 7.

You can also draw a quick picture to see which group has more:

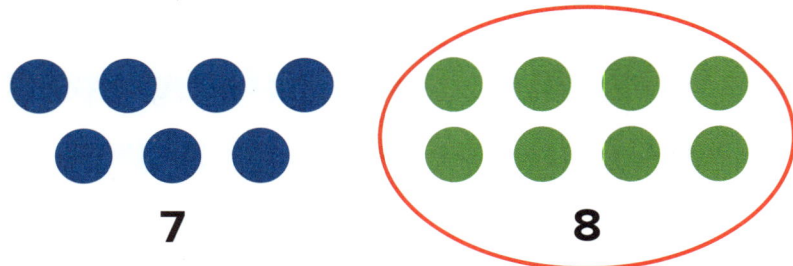

8 has *more than* 7.

8 is *greater than* 7.

PRACTICE: Now you try

Count each of the numbers in your head. Circle the number that is greater. Draw a picture to help you.

1. 2 or 3	**2.** 8 or 9
3. 6 or 5	**4.** 2 or 1

Compare Numbers

Jane has some flowers. The number of flowers she has is greater than 5 but less than 7. Sam has 8 flowers. Compare Jane's number of flowers to Sam's number of flowers. Who has more? Explain your thinking.

Math Vocabulary
- numbers
- compare
- more
- greater than
- less than

Did you find the question?	Who has more?	yes	no
Did you circle helpful numbers and words?	② ⟨in all⟩	yes	no
Did you use pictures, counters, or numbers to help you solve?	🍎🍎 2 apples	yes	no
Can you explain your thinking in words?	✏️	yes	no

Roll two dice. Compare the two numbers you rolled. Which is greater? Which is less? Remember what we call two numbers that are the same!

CCSS.Math.Content.K.CC.C.7

UNIT 3

CORE Counting and Base-Ten Concepts (Numbers 11–19)

Break Apart Numbers

UNPACK THE STANDARD
You will break apart numbers from 11 to 19 into tens and ones.

LEARN IT: You know about numbers to 10. Now let's look at numbers that come after 10. We will use a *ten frame*. A ten frame holds 10 counters.

Example: Look at the numbers shown in the ten frames below.

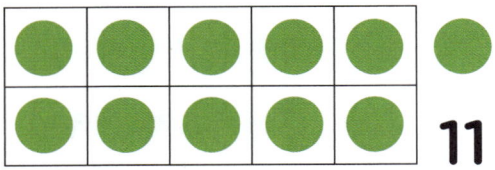

think! Count the number of counters in the ten frame. It is filled with 10 counters. So, we have 10 ones and 1 more. Count on one more from 10 to get 11!

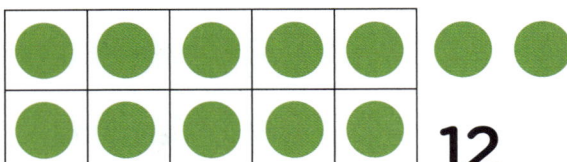

10 ones and 2 more

Count on from 10:

Say, "10, 11, 12."

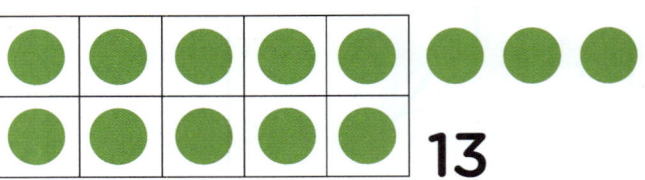

10 ones and 3 more

Count on from 10:

Say, "10, 11, 12, 13."

Break Apart Numbers

PRACTICE: Now you try

Use the ten frames to help you count. Write the number.

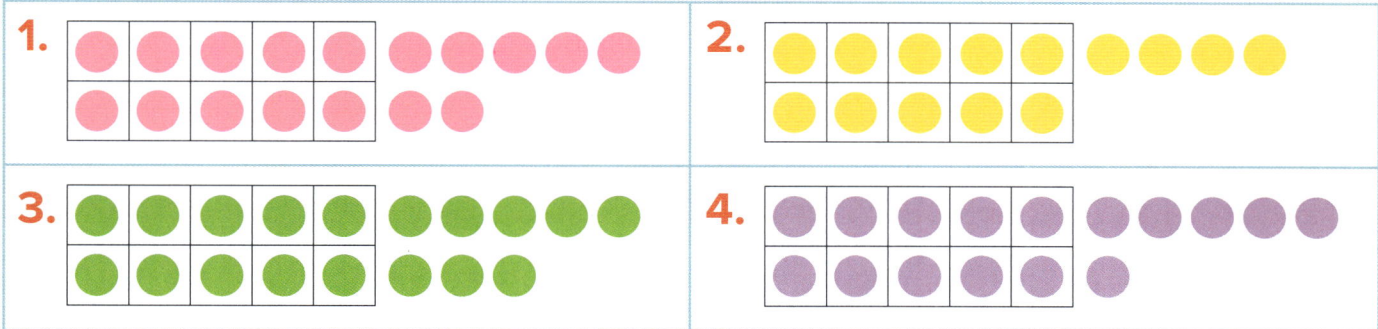

Zach has 16 toy cars. How can he break apart this number? Show your work and explain your thinking on a separate piece of paper.

Math Vocabulary
- break apart
- number
- ten
- ones
- ten frame

ACE IT TIME!

Did you find the question?	*How many more?*	yes / no
Did you circle helpful numbers and words?	② in all (circled)	yes / no
Did you use pictures, counters, or numbers to help you solve?	2 apples	yes / no
Can you explain your thinking in words?		yes / no

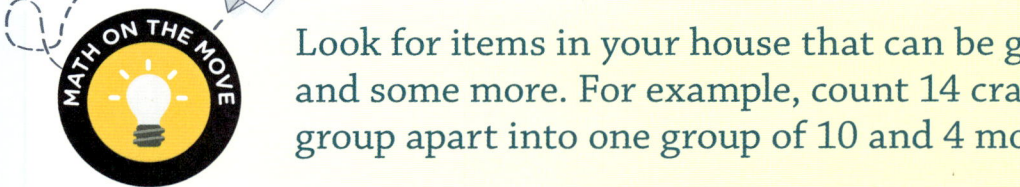

Look for items in your house that can be grouped into tens and some more. For example, count 14 crayons. Break the group apart into one group of 10 and 4 more ones!

Unit 3: CORE Counting and Base-Ten Concepts (Numbers 11–19)

Count 11–19

UNPACK THE STANDARD
You will count and write numbers 11 to 19.

LEARN IT: You know that numbers greater than 10 can be broken into 10 and more ones. Let's look at these numbers now without a ten frame.

Example: Count the books below and write the number.

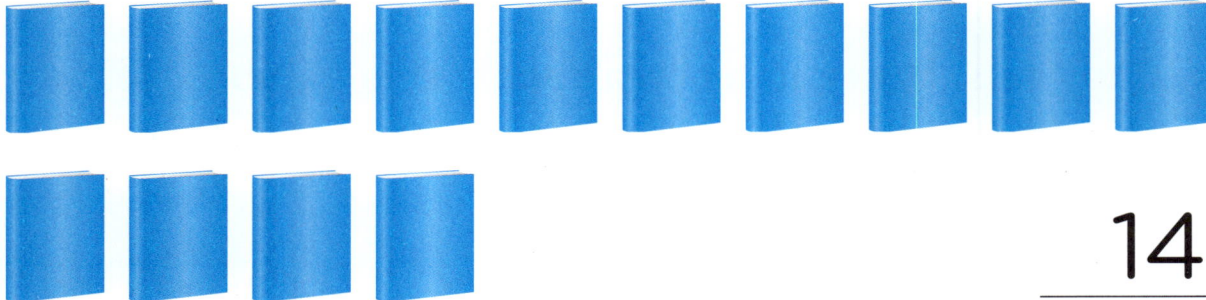

14

PRACTICE: Now you try

Count the snap cubes. Write the number.

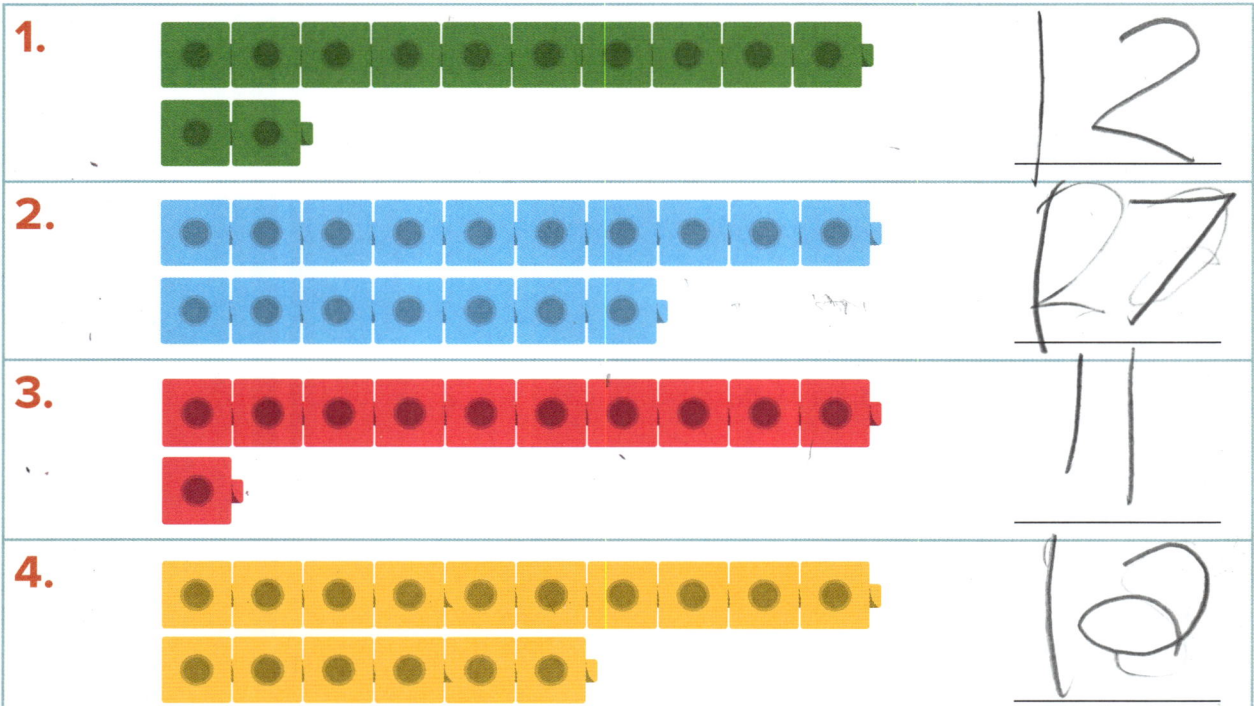

1. 12
2. 27
3. 11
4. 19

Count 11–19

Anna counts the books she sees. How many books are there? Count the books and write the number. Explain your thinking.

Math Vocabulary

count

number

ACE IT TIME!

Did you find the question?	*How many more?*	yes no
Did you circle helpful numbers and words?	② in all	yes no
Did you use pictures, counters, or numbers to help you solve?	2 apples	yes no
Can you explain your thinking in words?		yes no

MATH ON THE MOVE

Count out 19 pennies, buttons, or other small objects you can find at home. Write the number. Now take some away and count the number you have now. Write the number, and play again!

CCSS.Math.Content.K.CC.A.3, K.CC.B.4A–K.CC.B.4C

Unit 3: CORE Counting and Base-Ten Concepts (Numbers 11–19)

Count On

UNPACK THE STANDARD
You will count on from a given number between 11 and 19.

LEARN IT: You know how to count on from numbers 1 through 10. Use what you have learned to count on from numbers 11 through 19. Remember to count in order!

PRACTICE: Now you try

Count the flowers. Write the number in the box. Count on from that number.

1. [12], 13, 14, 15, 16, 17, 18, 19.

2. [15], 16, 17, 18, 19.

3. [17], 18, 19.

Count On

Count on from the number. Write the numbers.

4. 18, _____

5. 11, 12, _____, _____, _____, 16, _____, _____, 19

6. 14, _____, _____, _____, _____, 19

7. 13, _____, _____, _____, 17, _____, 19

8. 16, _____, _____, _____

Luis counts on from 11 to 19. He says "11, 12, 13, 15, 14, 16, 17, 18, 19." Is he correct? Explain your thinking.

ACE IT TIME!

Math Vocabulary
count on
numbers
order

Did you find the question?	*How many more?*	yes no
Did you circle helpful numbers and words?	② in all	yes no
Did you use pictures, counters, or numbers to help you solve?	2 apples	yes no
Can you explain your thinking in words?		yes no

Find a partner. Say a number 11 through 19. Your partner counts on from that number. Play again. Take turns being the "number picker" and the "counter." Remember to stop at 19!

Unit 3: CORE Counting and Base-Ten Concepts (Numbers 11–19)

Match Numbers and Names

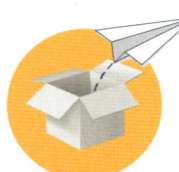

UNPACK THE STANDARD
You will match numbers 11 through 19 by counting how many are in the group.

LEARN IT: You can count to tell how many objects are in a group. You can match the number and the number name to the group of objects.

PRACTICE: Now you try

Count how many. Draw a line to match the number and the name.

1. 　　　　　　　　　　　　　　　　　　　　　11　eleven

2. 　　　　　　　　　　　　　　　　　　　　　17　seventeen

3. 　　　　　　　　　　　　　　　　　　　　　15　fifteen

4. 　　　　　　　　　　　　　　　　　　　　　13　thirteen

Match Numbers and Names

Count the counters. Tell how many.

5. 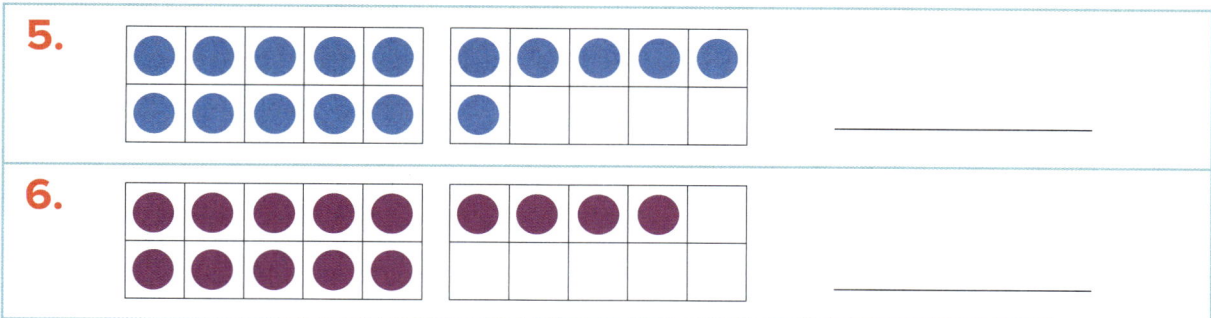 _____

6. _____

Kali counted 12 soccer balls. Draw the soccer balls. How many circles did you draw? Why? Explain your thinking.

ACE IT TIME!

Math Vocabulary

count
number

Did you find the question?	*How many more?*	yes no
Did you circle helpful numbers and words?	② in all	yes no
Did you use pictures, counters, or numbers to help you solve?	2 apples	yes no
Can you explain your thinking in words?		yes no

MATH ON THE MOVE

Adults, sort groups of apples, socks, crayons, or any other items you can find from 11–19. Then, write number names for each group on a piece of paper. Have your student match the number name to the group with that number of objects.

CCSS.Math.Content.K.CC.B.4A–K.CC.B.4C, CC.B.5

REVIEW

Stop and think about what you have learned.

Congratulations! You have finished the lessons for Units 2 and 3. You can count and order numbers 0 through 10. You can compare numbers to tell if they are greater than, less than, or equal. You can break apart numbers 11 through 19. You can count on with numbers between 0 and 19.

Now it's time to show your skills. Solve the problems below! Use what you have learned.

Activity Section 1

1. Count the snap cubes. Write the number.

   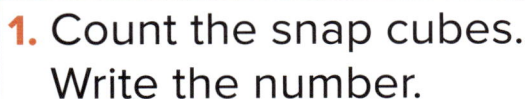

   _____ snap cubes

2. Count the snap cubes. Write the number. Count on.

   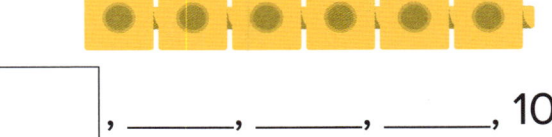

   [ ] , ____ , ____ , ____ , 10

3. How many are there?

   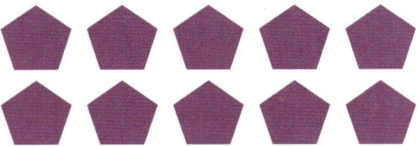

   _____

4. How many are there?

   _____

5. Count each group. Write the number. Circle the group that is greater.

   ____   ____

6. Count the objects in each group. Circle the group that is less.

   ____   ____

7. Circle the greater number.

4   3

8. Circle the number that is less.

9   7

Activity Section 2

1. Count the counters.

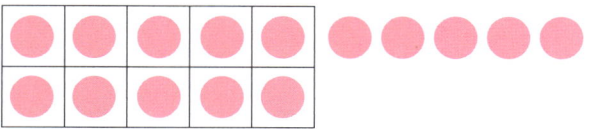

_____

2. Count the counters.

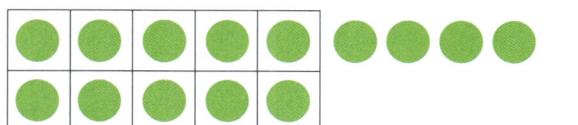

_____

3. How many are there?

_____

4. How many are there?

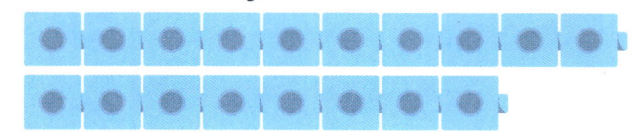

_____

5. Count on.

16, _____, _____, 19

6. Count on.

14, _____, _____, _____, 18, _____

7. Count on.

15, _____, _____, _____, _____

8. Count on.

13, _____, 15, _____, 17, _____, 19

9. How many are there?

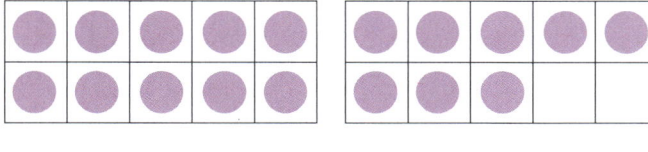

_____

10. How many are there?

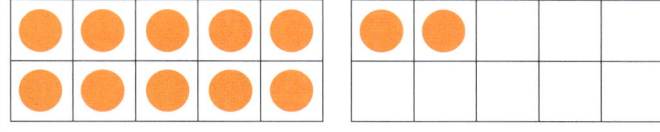

_____

UNDERSTAND

Stop and think about what you have learned.

Use what you know about breaking apart numbers to solve the problem below.

Activity Section

Kate collects stickers. She keeps them in a sticker book. Her sister Lee collects stickers, too. She put her stickers on the next page of the sticker book. Count how many stickers both girls have. Who has more? Explain how you know.

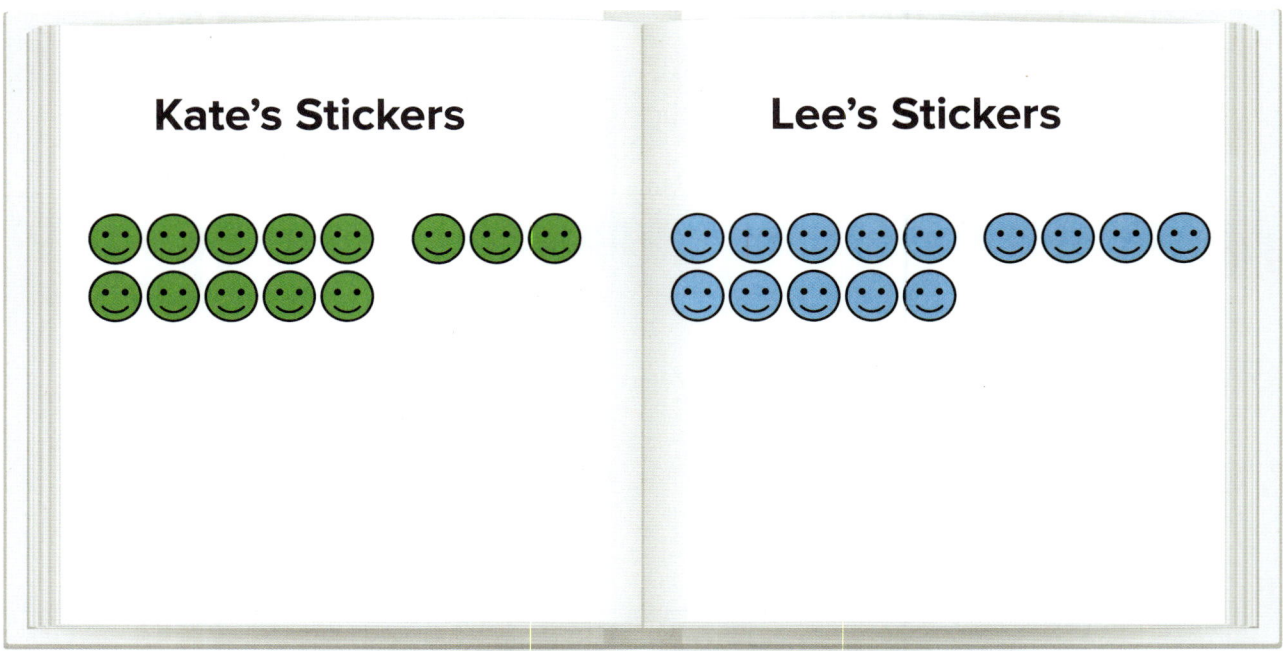

Kate's page has _____ stickers. It has 10 ones and _____ more.

Lee's page has _____ stickers. It has 10 ones and _____ more.

_____ has more stickers.

DISCOVER

Stop and think about what you have learned.

We compare numbers all the time in real life.

Activity Section

Andy has some balloons. He has 1 more than 6. Jen has some balloons too. She has 1 more than 5.

1. How many balloons does Andy have? Draw a picture to solve.

2. How many balloons does Jen have? Draw a picture to solve.

3. Who has the greater amount of balloons? Explain your thinking.

UNIT 4
CORE Addition and Subtraction Concepts

What Is Addition?

UNPACK THE STANDARD
You will model and solve addition problems.

LEARN IT: You know how to count objects in a group. But what if you put two groups together? That is called adding, or *addition*. You can add one group of objects to another.

Example: 2 frogs sit on a log. 1 more frog hops on. How many frogs are there now?

Count the frogs in the first group.

Count the frogs there are in the second group.

Add the groups together to find how many frogs there are in all. You can use counters or other small objects at home to help!

2 and 1 is 3

2 + 1 = 3

Do you see the plus sign? It means to add!

Say, "2 plus 1 equals 3."

What Is Addition?

PRACTICE: Now you try

Count each group of snap cubes. Add them together. Write the numbers.

1.

_____ and _____ is _____

_____ + _____ = _____

1 child was sitting on the swings. 3 more children joined him. How many children were on the swings? Draw a picture or use counters to help you. Show your work and explain your thinking on a separate piece of paper.

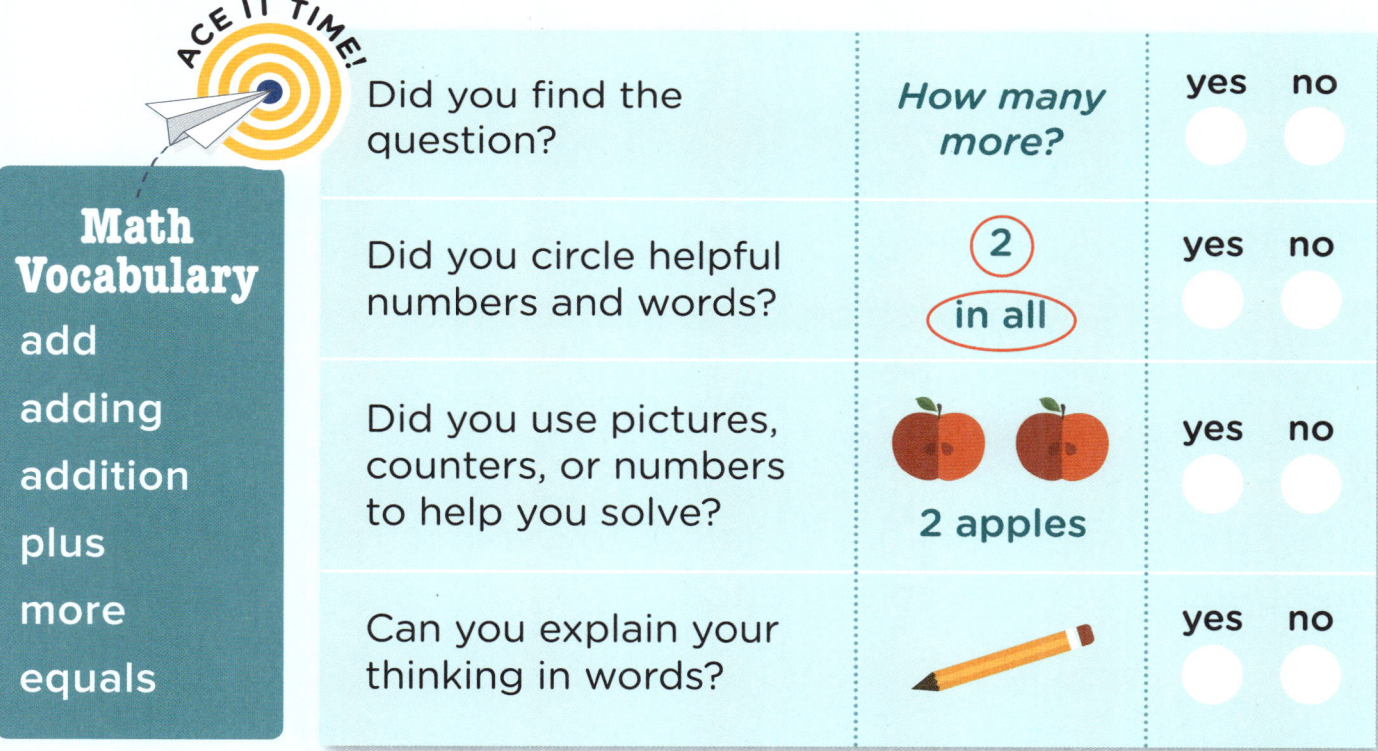

Math Vocabulary
add
adding
addition
plus
more
equals

Lights, camera, action! Act out addition problems like the ones in this lesson. You can use friends, toys, or other objects you find around the house to make groups! For example, 2 people are in the kitchen. Then, 1 more person comes in. How many people are in the kitchen? Act it out!

Unit 4: CORE Addition and Subtraction Concepts

Practice Adding up to 5

 **UNPACK THE STANDARD**
You will practice adding numbers up to 5.

LEARN IT: You know that addition means putting two groups together. Let's practice adding numbers up to 5.

Example: Add the cubes.

Put the groups together to add. Write the numbers as an addition problem. Count how many in all.

1 + 3 = 4

think!
Put the blue cube and the pink cubes together to make a "train" of 4 cubes!

Hint: 1 + 3 = 4 is an addition sentence! It is like a sentence with numbers.

PRACTICE: Now you try

Draw the groups of cubes together to make a train. Write the numbers in an addition sentence.

1.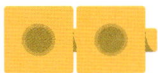

   _____ + _____ = _____

2.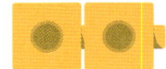

   _____ + _____ = _____

130   CCSS.Math.Content.K.OA.A.5

Practice Adding up to 5

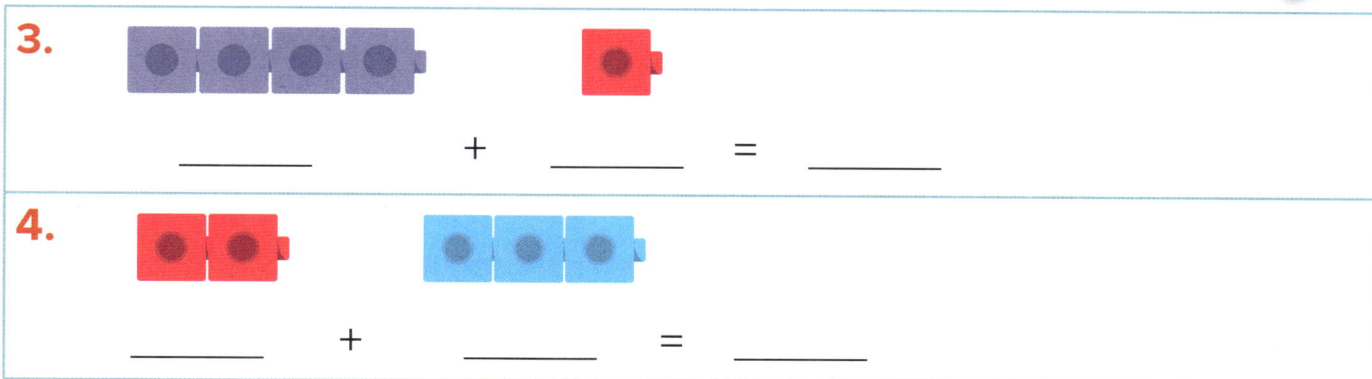

3. ____ + ____ = ____

4. ____ + ____ = ____

Will has 2 video games. His brother James has 2 video games. How many video games do they have together? Draw a picture to solve. Show your work and explain your thinking on a separate piece of paper.

ACE IT TIME!

Math Vocabulary
- add
- plus
- equals
- more
- together

Did you find the question?	*How many more?*	yes no
Did you circle helpful numbers and words?	② in all	yes no
Did you use pictures, counters, or numbers to help you solve?	2 apples	yes no
Can you explain your thinking in words?		yes no

Math on the Move

Tell an addition story about adding one group of objects to another. Find the answer. For example, "There were 3 dogs in the park. 2 more dogs came. There were 5 dogs in all."

Unit 4: CORE Addition and Subtraction Concepts

Make a Ten

UNPACK THE STANDARD
You will make 10 by adding two numbers.

LEARN IT: You know that adding means putting two groups together. Let's look at numbers that add together to make 10.

Example: Look at the snap cube train below. How many green cubes do you see? How many red cubes should you add to make 10? Write the numbers to make an addition sentence.

$9 + 1 = 10$

think! Count on from 9 to 10. How many numbers did you say? One! We can add 1 red cube to make 10 cubes in all.

There are other ways to make 10.
Use the practice problems below to find all the ways to make 10.
Can you see a pattern?

PRACTICE: Now you try

Draw squares on to the snap cube trains to make 10. Write the number sentence.

1.

$8 + \underline{} = 10$

2.
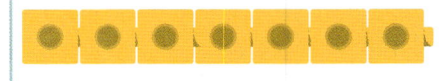
$\underline{} + \underline{} = 10$

3.
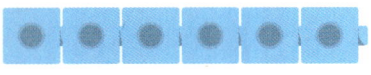
$\underline{} + \underline{} = 10$

4.

$\underline{} + \underline{} = 10$

Make a Ten

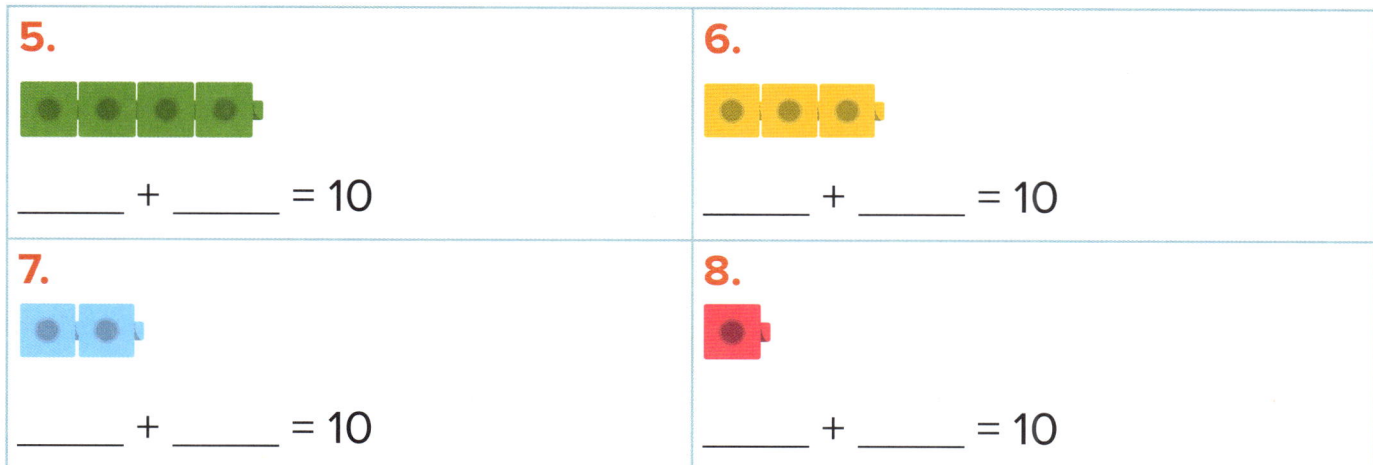

5. ____ + ____ = 10

6. ____ + ____ = 10

7. ____ + ____ = 10

8. ____ + ____ = 10

What if you had zero snap cubes? How many cubes would you need to add to make 10? Draw a picture to solve. Show your work and explain your thinking on a separate piece of paper.

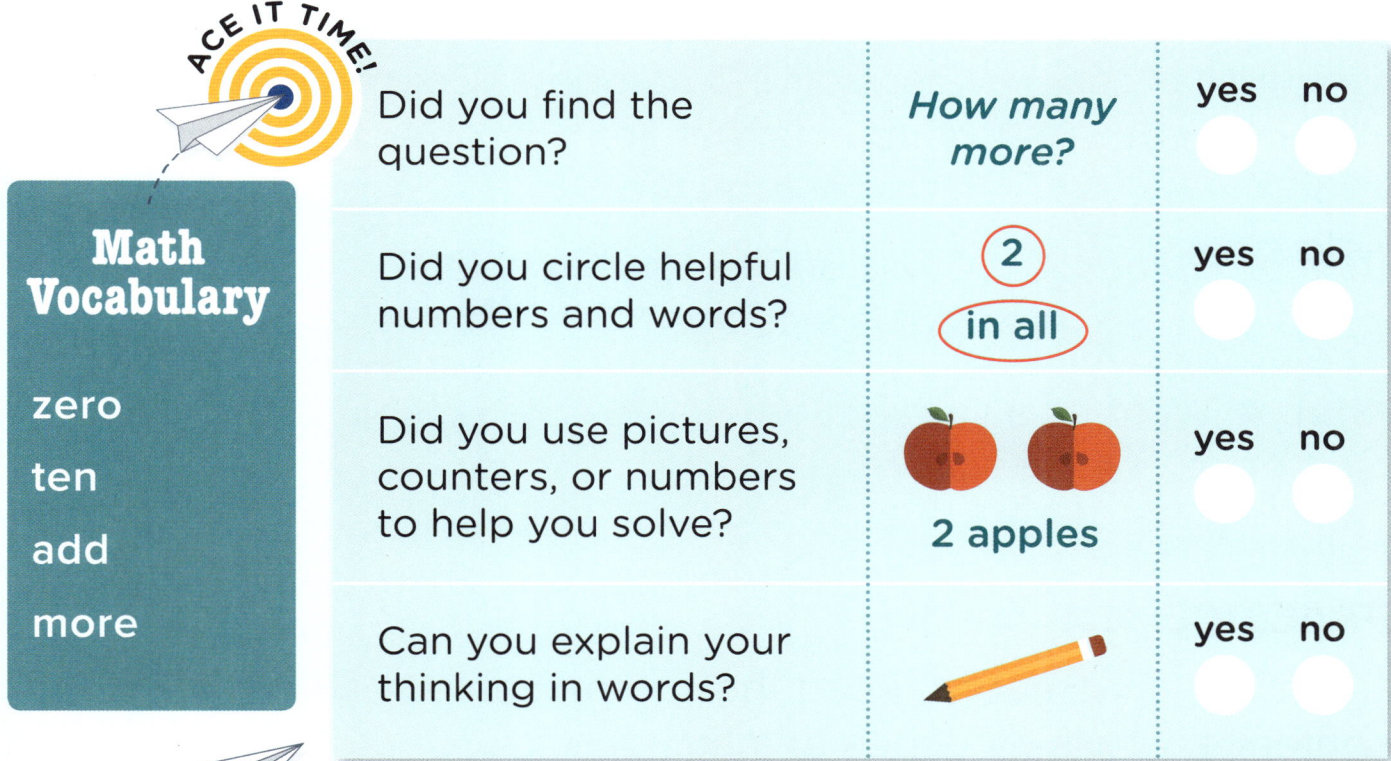

Pick a number 0–9. How many more do you need to add to get to 10? Practice counting on to help!

CCSS.Math.Content.K.OA.A.3, OA.A.4

Unit 4: CORE Addition and Subtraction Concepts

What Is Subtraction?

UNPACK THE STANDARD
You will model and solve subtraction problems.

LEARN IT: You know that addition is putting groups together. *Subtraction* is the opposite of addition! It means taking apart or taking away from a group.

Example: 4 puppies were playing at the dog park. 1 of the puppies went home. How many puppies were left at the dog park?

Step 1: Count all of the objects in the group. *This group has 4 puppies.*	**Step 2:** Cross off the number of objects that are being subtracted. *Cross off the 1 puppy that is leaving!*	**Step 3:** Count how many objects are left. *There are 3 puppies left.*

Step 4: Write as a subtraction sentence. $4 - 1 = 3$

think! We say:
"4 take away 1 equals 3"
"4 minus 1 equals 3"
"4 subtract 1 equals 3"

PRACTICE: Now you try

Count the snap cubes. Read the subtraction sentence. Cross off cubes to match the sentence. Complete the subtraction sentence.

think! How many should you cross off? How many are left?

1. $4 - 2 = $ _____

2. $3 - 2 = $ _____

CCSS.Math.Content.K.OA.A.1, OA.A.2

What Is Subtraction?

Izzy has 4 friendship bracelets. She gives 3 bracelets away to her friends. How many bracelets does she have left? Draw a picture and write a subtraction sentence to help you solve. Explain your thinking.

ACE IT TIME!

Math Vocabulary
- subtract
- minus
- take away
- equals
- left

Did you find the question?	*How many more?*	yes	no
Did you circle helpful numbers and words?	② ⟨in all⟩	yes	no
Did you use pictures, counters, or numbers to help you solve?	2 apples	yes	no
Can you explain your thinking in words?	✏️	yes	no

Subtract as you eat! Use small snacks such as crackers, pretzels, or berries. Start with 5. Eat 1. How many do you have left? How would you say and write this as a subtraction problem? Keep subtracting until you get to 0!

Unit 4: CORE Addition and Subtraction Concepts

Practice Subtracting with Numbers 0–5

UNPACK THE STANDARD
You will practice subtracting numbers from 0 to 5.

LEARN IT: You know that subtraction means taking apart or taking objects from a group. Let's practice subtracting numbers from 0 to 5.

Example: 5 birds sat on a wire. 3 birds flew away. How many birds were left? Cross off the birds that flew away to count how many are left. Write a subtraction sentence.

_____ — _____ = _____

PRACTICE: Now you try

Count the snap cubes. Cross off cubes to match the subtraction sentence. Write the numbers.

1.	2 – 1 = ____	2.	3 – 1 = ____
3.	5 – 2 = ____	4.	2 – 1 = ____
5.	5 – 4 = ____	6.	3 – 0 = ____
7.	4 – 1 = ____	8.	4 – 3 = ____

Practice Subtracting with Numbers 0–5

A.J.'s mom gave him 2 slices of watermelon. He ate both of them. What subtraction sentence can you write for this problem? How many watermelon slices are left? Draw a picture and write the subtraction sentence to solve. Explain your thinking.

ACE IT TIME!

Math Vocabulary
- take away
- subtract
- left

Did you find the question?	*How many more?*	yes	no
Did you circle helpful numbers and words?	② ⬭in all⬬	yes	no
Did you use pictures, counters, or numbers to help you solve?	🍎🍎 2 apples	yes	no
Can you explain your thinking in words?	✏️	yes	no

Find 5 small objects around the house like pennies, buttons, or paper clips. Take some away. How many are left? Write a subtraction sentence.

UNIT 5

CORE Counting and Number Set Concepts (Numbers up to 20 and Beyond)

Count Objects up to 20

UNPACK THE STANDARD
You will count objects up to 20 and write the number.

LEARN IT: Now that you have worked with numbers 0 through 19, what comes next? Yes, 20! Let's look at different ways to show *20*. Remember to touch each object as you count!

Example: Count the counters in the ten frames. Write how many there are.

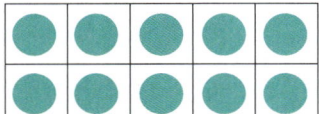 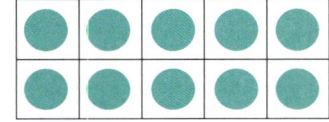

20 twenty

think! There are two full ten frames. 10 and 10 make 20!

PRACTICE: Now you try

Count the objects. Write the number.

1. Count the dots on the ladybug.  _____

2.        _____

3.      _____

Count Objects up to 20

4. 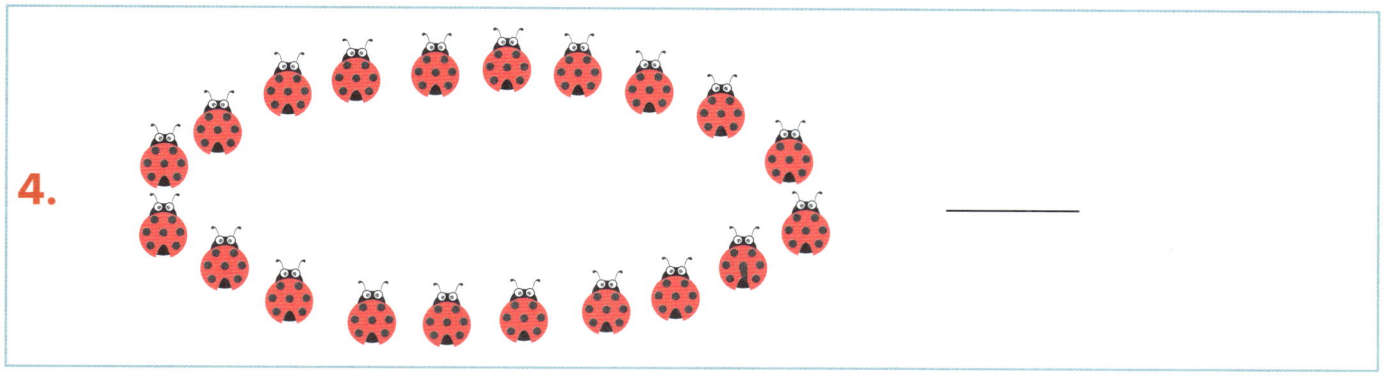 _____

Does the picture below show 20? Why or why not? Explain your thinking on a separate piece of paper.

Math Vocabulary

count

20

twenty

ten frame

ACE IT TIME!

Did you find the question?	*How many more?*	yes no
Did you circle helpful numbers and words?	②　in all	yes no
Did you use pictures, counters, or numbers to help you solve?	2 apples	yes no
Can you explain your thinking in words?		yes no

Go on a treasure hunt! Ask an adult to hide from 10 to 20 small items such as rocks, shells, or coins in a large bowl of uncooked rice. Dig until you find the total number of items hidden. Write the number in the rice for fun!

Unit 5: CORE Counting and Number Set Concepts

Count to 50 by Ones

UNPACK THE STANDARD
You will count to 50.

LEARN IT: You know how to count to 20. Now let's keep going! What numbers come after 20?

Look at the chart. Touch each number as you count out loud from 1 to 50. Circle the number 50.

1	2	3	4	5	6	7	8	9	10
11	12	13	14	15	16	17	18	19	20
21	22	23	24	25	26	27	28	29	30
31	32	33	34	35	36	37	38	39	40
41	42	43	44	45	46	47	48	49	(50)

think!
Look at the numbers in the chart. Do you see a pattern? Now listen to yourself as you count. Do you *hear* a pattern?

PRACTICE: Now you try

Use the chart to count on from the given number. End at 50.

1. Circle the number 25. Count on to 50. Draw a box around the number 50.

1	2	3	4	5	6	7	8	9	10
11	12	13	14	15	16	17	18	19	20
21	22	23	24	25	26	27	28	29	30
31	32	33	34	35	36	37	38	39	40
41	42	43	44	45	46	47	48	49	50

Count to 50 by Ones

2. Circle the number 39. Count on to 50. Draw a box around the number 50.

1	2	3	4	5	6	7	8	9	10
11	12	13	14	15	16	17	18	19	20
21	22	23	24	25	26	27	28	29	30
31	32	33	34	35	36	37	38	39	40
41	42	43	44	45	46	47	48	49	50

Hailey was counting to 50. She counted on from 42. She said "42, 43, 44, 45, 46, 47, 49, 50." Where did she make her mistake? Show your work and explain your thinking on a piece of paper.

ACE IT TIME!

Math Vocabulary
counting on
numbers
order
50

Did you find the question?	How many more?	yes no
Did you circle helpful numbers and words?	2 in all	yes no
Did you use pictures, counters, or numbers to help you solve?	2 apples	yes no
Can you explain your thinking in words?		yes no

Use one of the number charts in this lesson. Close your eyes and point to a number. Open your eyes. Count on from that number to 50!

CCSS.Math.Content.K.CC.A.1

Unit 5: CORE Counting and Number Set Concepts

Count to 100 by Ones and Tens

UNPACK THE STANDARD
You will count to 100.

LEARN IT: Now that you can count to 50, let's keep going to 100! In this lesson, we will count to 100 by *ones and tens.*

Look at the chart. Touch each number as you count out loud from 1 to 100. Circle every number that ends in 0.

1	2	3	4	5	6	7	8	9	10
11	12	13	14	15	16	17	18	19	20
21	22	23	24	25	26	27	28	29	30
31	32	33	34	35	36	37	38	39	40
41	42	43	44	45	46	47	48	49	50
51	52	53	54	55	56	57	58	59	60
61	62	63	64	65	66	67	68	69	70
71	72	73	74	75	76	77	78	79	80
81	82	83	84	85	86	87	88	89	90
91	92	93	94	95	96	97	98	99	100

think! Look at the numbers you circled. Say them out loud as you count by tens to 100: "10, 20, 30, 40, 50, 60, 70, 80, 90, 100!"

The numbers you circled are called tens. They end in zero. You can show these numbers as groups of 10. Let's practice.

PRACTICE: Now you try

Use the groups of tens to tell how many there are. Write the number.

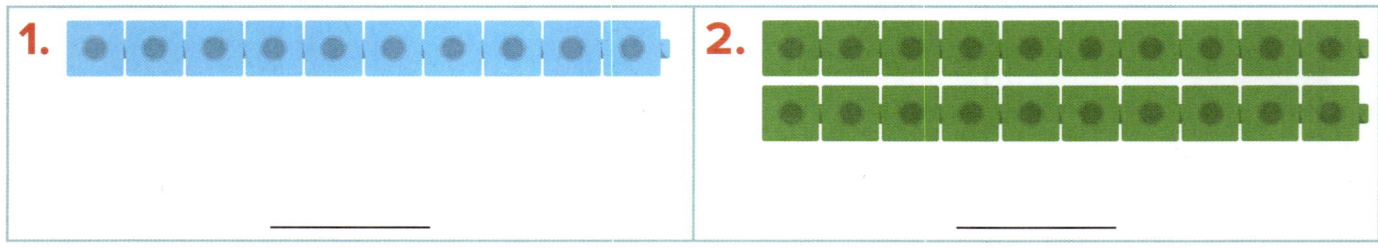

1. _____
2. _____

CCSS.Math.Content.K.CC.A.1

Count to 100 by Ones and Tens

Count by tens. Write the number.

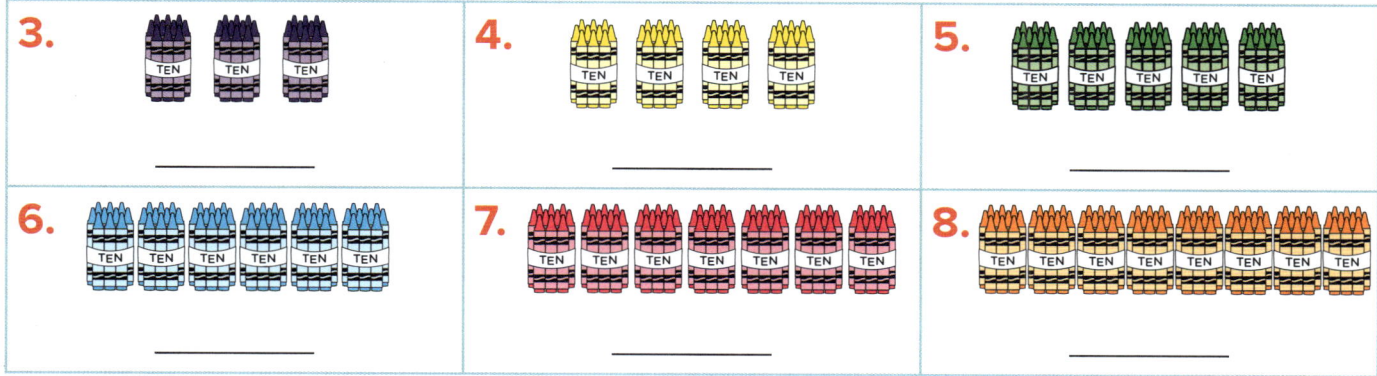

Do you see the pattern in the numbers above? What two numbers will come next if you keep counting by tens? How do you know? Show your work and explain your thinking on a piece of paper.

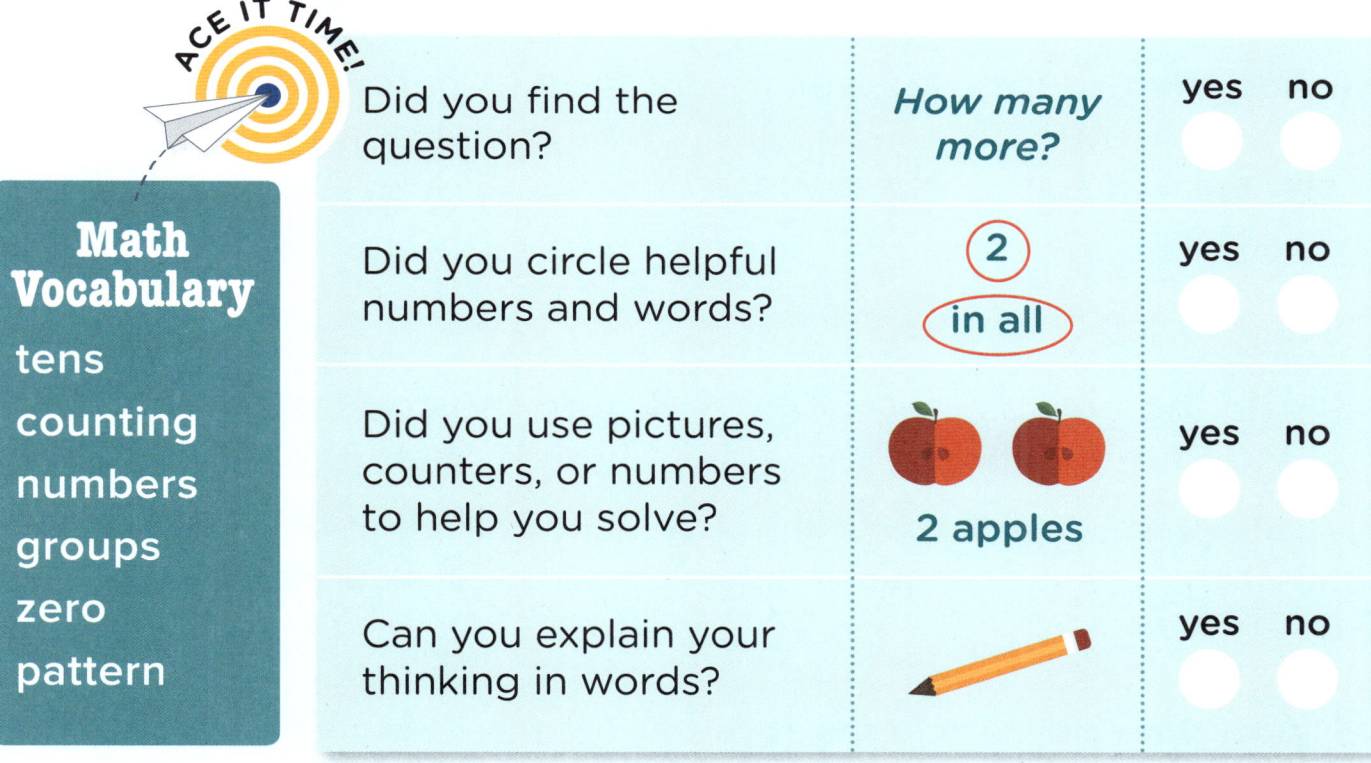

Math Vocabulary
- tens
- counting
- numbers
- groups
- zero
- pattern

Did you know that a dime is worth ten cents? Ask a parent or adult helper to find some dimes around the house. Practice counting by tens with dimes!

REVIEW

Stop and think about what you have learned.

Congratulations! You have finished the lessons for Units 4 and 5. You can add numbers up to 10. You can find ways to make a ten. You can also subtract numbers from a group. You also know about numbers up to 20, and can compare and order those numbers. You even know how to count to 50 by ones, and 100 by ones and tens!

Now it's time to show your skills. Solve the problems below! Use what you have learned.

Activity Section 1

1. Add the groups together. Write the numbers.

_____ and _____ is _____

_____ + _____ = _____

2. Add the groups together. Write the numbers.

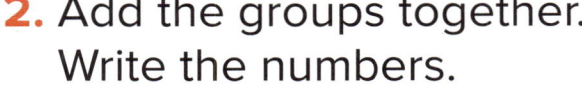

_____ and _____ is _____

_____ + _____ = _____

3. Add the groups together. Write the numbers.

_____ and _____ is _____

_____ + _____ = _____

4. Add the counters in the ten frame. Write the numbers.

_____ + _____ = _____

5. Add the counters in the ten frame. Write the numbers.

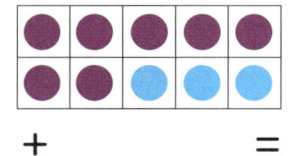

_____ + _____ = _____

6. Count. Cross off to subtract. Write the numbers.

_____ − 4 = _____

Stop and Think! Review **Units 4–5**

7. Count. Cross off to subtract. Write the numbers.

_____ − 3 = _____

8. Count. Cross off to subtract. Write the numbers.

_____ − 7 = _____

Activity Section 2

1. Count the objects. _____

2. Count the objects. _____

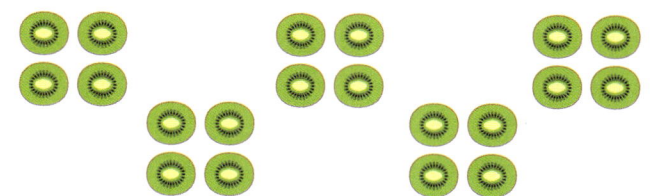

3. Circle each of these numbers on the chart. Count on to 100. Touch each number as you count.

36   48   63   79   90

1	2	3	4	5	6	7	8	9	10
11	12	13	14	15	16	17	18	19	20
21	22	23	24	25	26	27	28	29	30
31	32	33	34	35	36	37	38	39	40
41	42	43	44	45	46	47	48	49	50
51	52	53	54	55	56	57	58	59	60
61	62	63	64	65	66	67	68	69	70
71	72	73	74	75	76	77	78	79	80
81	82	83	84	85	86	87	88	89	90
91	92	93	94	95	96	97	98	99	100

4. Count by tens. _____

5. Count by tens. _____

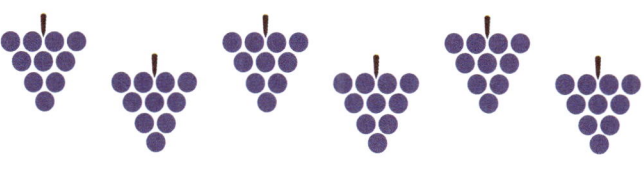

UNDERSTAND

Stop and think about what you have learned.

Use what you know about counting to 100 by ones for this activity. Be sure you are counting in order!

Activity Section

Help! There are numbers missing on the hundred chart! Can you fill them in?

1	2	3	4		6	7	8	9	10
11	12	13		15	16	17	18	19	20
21	22	23	24	25	26			29	30
31	32		34	35	36	37	38	39	40
41	42	43	44	45		47	48	49	50
51	52	53	54	55	56	57	58	59	
61			64	65	66	67	68	69	70
71	72	73	74	75	76	77		79	80
	82	83	84	85	86	87	88	89	90
91	92	93	94	95	96	97	98		100

DISCOVER

Stop and think about what you have learned.

Counting by tens is a skill that you will use very often in your life. Here you will make your own groups of ten to count a large amount of objects!

Activity Section

Circle groups of ten gumballs in the jar. Write how many gumballs are in the jar.

There are _____ gumballs in the jar.

UNIT 6

CORE Geometry Concepts

Name that Shape

UNPACK THE STANDARD
You will identify two-dimensional shapes.

LEARN IT: Let's learn the names of some different shapes and what makes them different from each other. These shapes are called two-dimensional shapes, or "flat" shapes.

think! Use your finger to trace the red sides of each shape as you learn about them. Stop at each corner! A corner is where two sides meet. It is also called a vertex.

This is a circle.

It is a round shape made up of a curved line. It has 0 sides and 0 corners!

This is a triangle.

It has 3 sides and 3 corners.

This is a rectangle.

It has 4 sides and 4 corners. The two opposite sides are the same length!

This is a square.

It has 4 sides and 4 corners. All sides are the same length!

This is a hexagon.

It has 6 sides and 6 corners.

Name that Shape

PRACTICE: Now you try

Draw a line around all of the shapes that are named below.

Hint: The size and direction of the shape does not matter!

2. Rectangles	3. Hexagons
1. Circles	
4. Triangles	5. Squares

Kyra is thinking of a shape. It has 6 sides and 6 corners. What shape is she thinking of? Draw the shape. Show your work and explain your thinking on a piece of paper.

ACE IT TIME!

Math Vocabulary
- shape
- sides
- corners
- rectangle
- square
- triangle
- hexagon
- circle

	How many more?	yes no
Did you find the question?		○ ○
Did you circle helpful numbers and words?	2 in all	○ ○
Did you use pictures, counters, or numbers to help you solve?	2 apples	○ ○
Can you explain your thinking in words?		○ ○

Go on a shape hunt! Look for shapes all around your house, in your yard, and while riding in the car! Practice drawing and counting the sides and corners of the shapes you find.

CCSS.Math.Content.K.G.A.2, K.G.A.3

Unit 6: CORE Geometry Concepts

Compare Shapes

UNPACK THE STANDARD
You will compare two-dimensional shapes.

LEARN IT: You have learned about 5 different types of shapes. Let's look more closely as to how these shapes are alike and how they are different.

Example: Compare a square with a triangle. Look at the pictures below.

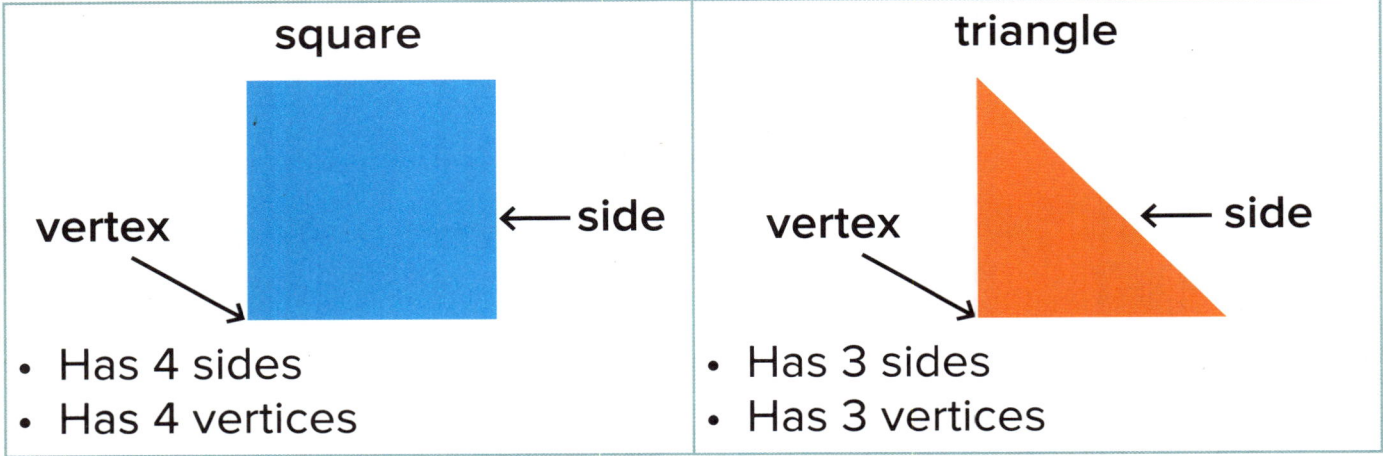

- Has 4 sides
- Has 4 vertices

- Has 3 sides
- Has 3 vertices

Hint: "Vertices" means more than one vertex. And a vertex is a corner!

PRACTICE: Now you try

1. Color all the shapes that have 3 vertices and 3 sides BLUE.
   Color all the shapes that have 4 vertices and 4 sides RED.
   Color all the shapes that have 6 vertices and 6 sides GREEN.

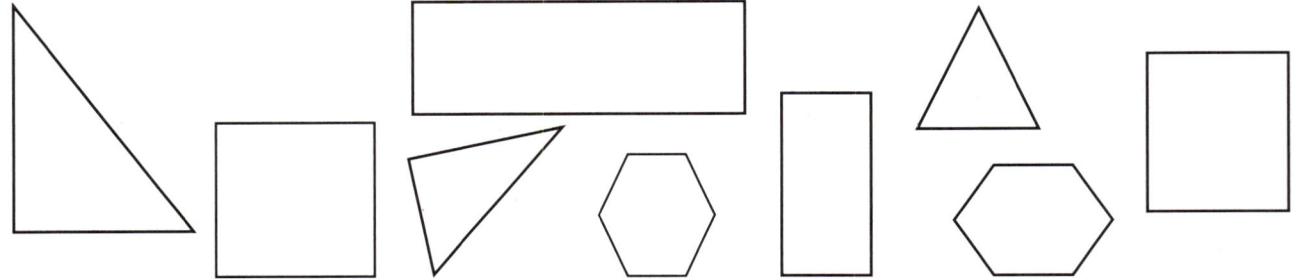

Compare Shapes

Tell an adult how the two shapes are alike. Then tell an adult how they are different.

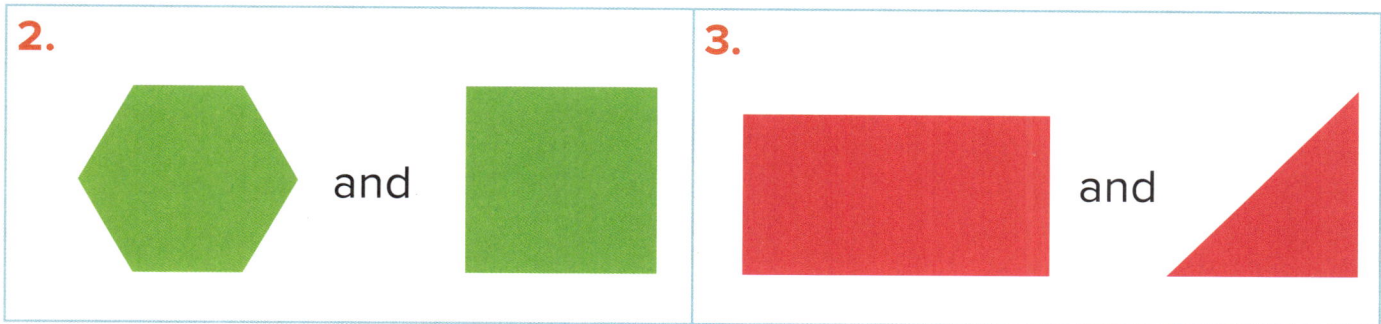

2. and

3. and

Compare a square and a rectangle. How are they alike? How are they different? Show your work and explain your thinking on a separate piece of paper.

ACE IT TIME!

Math Vocabulary
- square
- rectangle
- sides
- vertices
- corners
- alike
- different

Did you find the question?	*How many more?*	yes no
Did you circle helpful numbers and words?	② in all	yes no
Did you use pictures, counters, or numbers to help you solve?	2 apples	yes no
Can you explain your thinking in words?		yes no

MATH ON THE MOVE

When you are walking in your neighborhood, what shapes do you see? What shape is a stop sign? What shape are traffic lights? What shape is the sidewalk? Draw a picture of all the shapes you see!

Unit 6: CORE Geometry Concepts

Cylinder, Cone, Sphere, and Cube

UNPACK THE STANDARD
You will identify three-dimensional shapes.

LEARN IT: A three-dimensional shape is called a *solid*. Some of these solids have flat surfaces. They can stack, slide, or roll. Let's look at some of these solids.

A **cylinder** has 1 curved surface.

It has 2 flat surfaces.

It can stack when it stands on one of its flat sides.

It can roll when you lay it down.

A **cone** has 1 curved surface.

It has 1 flat surface.

It cannot be stacked.

It can slide.

A **sphere** has 0 flat surfaces.

It is round all around.

It can roll like a ball.

A **cube** has 6 flat surfaces.

It can stack and slide like a box.

Cylinder, Cone, Sphere, and Cube

PRACTICE: Now you try

Look at the three-dimensional solids below. Draw a line to the names that match.

cone   sphere   cylinder   cube

Jeremy collected several sphere-shaped objects from around his house. Name some objects he may have collected. Show your work and explain your thinking on a separate piece of paper.

Math Vocabulary
- sphere
- solids
- roll

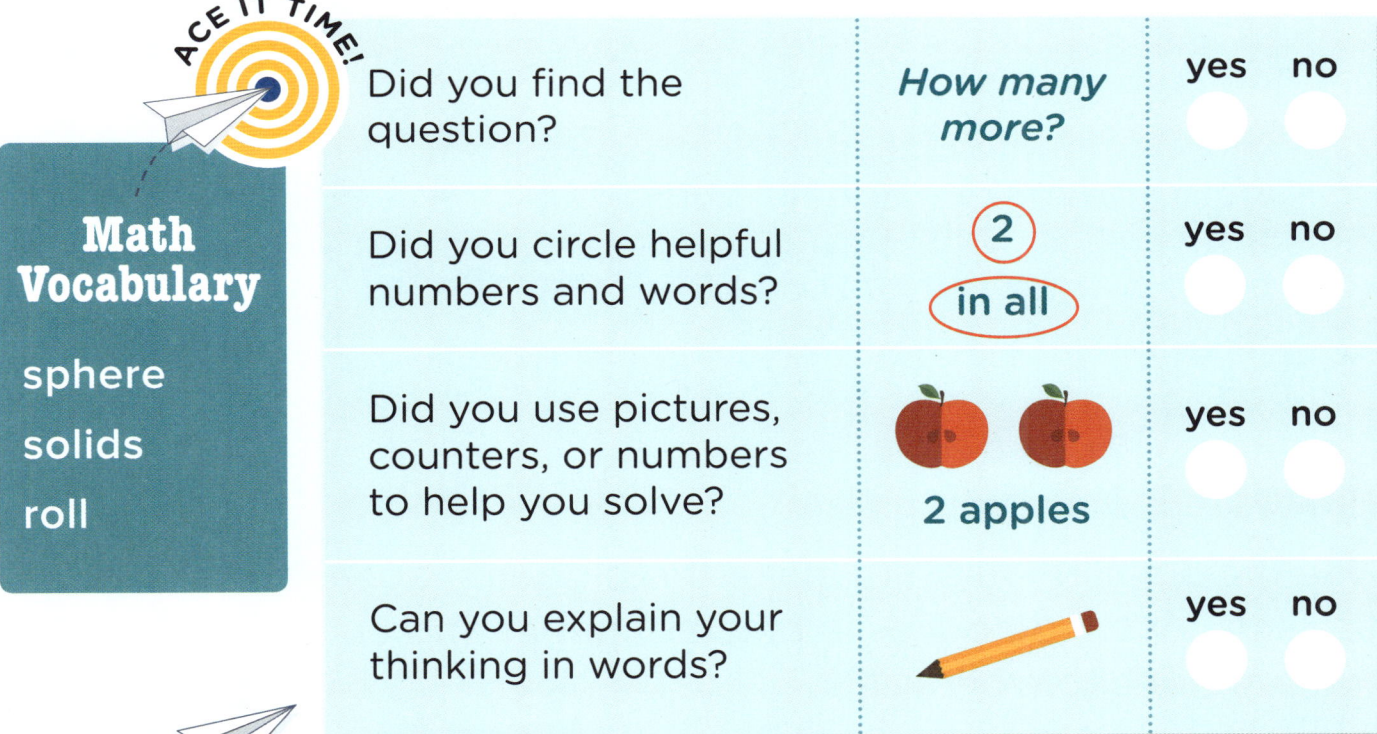

	Did you find the question?		yes no
	Did you circle helpful numbers and words?	How many more? ② in all	yes no
	Did you use pictures, counters, or numbers to help you solve?	2 apples	yes no
	Can you explain your thinking in words?		yes no

Look for three-dimensional solid shapes around the house! You can find a lot of cylinders in the kitchen.

CCSS.Math.Content.K.G.A.3, K.G.B.4

Unit 6: CORE Geometry Concepts

Build Shapes

UNPACK THE STANDARD
You will put together shapes to make bigger shapes.

LEARN IT: Let's review some of the two-dimensional shapes you have already learned. You can use them to make bigger shapes.

Example: Can you combine these 2 triangles to make a rectangle?

Imagine moving these triangles around. Flip the second triangle upside down and place it on top of the first triangle. You have made a rectangle!

think! What about a three-dimensional solid? Could you make a sphere out of modeling clay? Could you make a cube out of modeling clay and toothpicks?

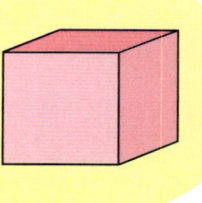

PRACTICE: Now you try

Use the smaller shape to make the bigger shape. You can trace the smaller shape out on a piece of paper and cut it out so you have shapes to work with!

1. Make a rectangle using these squares. Draw the rectangle.

Build Shapes

2. Make a square using these triangles. Draw the square.

3. Make a large square using these squares. Draw the square.

The shape shown here is called a trapezoid. Can you make a hexagon using 2 trapezoids? Remember, a hexagon has 6 sides! How do you know the new shape you made is a hexagon? Show your work and explain your thinking on a separate piece of paper.

ACE IT TIME!

Math Vocabulary
- trapezoid
- hexagon
- shape
- combine
- sides

Did you find the question?	*How many more?*	yes no
Did you circle helpful numbers and words?	② in all	yes no
Did you use pictures, counters, or numbers to help you solve?	🍎🍎 2 apples	yes no
Can you explain your thinking in words?	✏️	yes no

MATH ON THE MOVE
Ask an adult for some modeling clay and toothpicks. Practice making three-dimensional solids! Can you make a cube? How about a cone, cylinder, or sphere?

Unit 6: CORE Geometry Concepts

Where Is It?

UNPACK THE STANDARD
You will describe the position of an object.

LEARN IT: You know the names of several two- and three-dimensional shapes. Now let's practice describing the position of the shape by telling where it is.

Example: Look at the shapes. Describe the position of each shape.

The cube is **in front of** the hexagon.
The hexagon is **behind** the cube.

The cube is **beside** the cylinder.
Or, the cylinder is **next to** the cube.

The cylinder is **above** the triangle.
The triangle is **below** the cylinder.

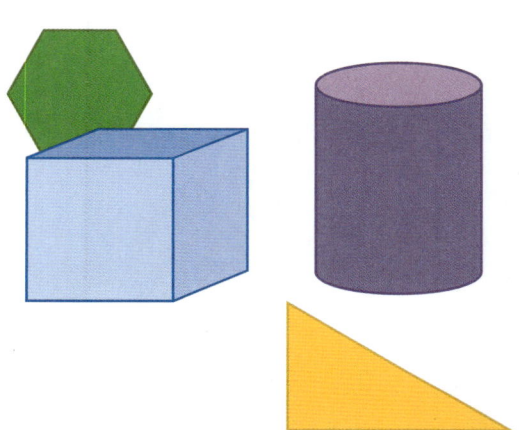

PRACTICE: Now you try

1. Circle the shape that is **below** the triangle. Name the shape. Draw an X on the shape that is **next to** the triangle. Name the shape.

156   CCSS.Math.Content.K.G.A.1

Where Is It?

2. Circle the shape that is **beside** the cylinder. Name the shape. Draw an X on the shape that is **above** the cylinder. Name the shape.

Lunch time! Abby, Brent, and Carlos lined up for lunch in this order. Using the words "in front of" and "behind," describe the position of each child as he or she stands in line. Show your work and explain your thinking on a piece of paper.

ACE IT TIME!

Math Vocabulary
in front of
behind
order

	Did you find the question?	How many more?	yes no
	Did you circle helpful numbers and words?	② in all	yes no
	Did you use pictures, counters, or numbers to help you solve?	2 apples	yes no
	Can you explain your thinking in words?		yes no

Practice describing the position of objects at home. For example, open the refrigerator in your kitchen. Can you describe where different foods are using the words next to, beside, behind, in front of, above, and below?

CCSS.Math.Content.K.G.A.1

UNIT 7: CORE Measurement and Data Concepts

Describe Objects

UNPACK THE STANDARD
You will describe objects based on their length and height.

LEARN IT: You have learned about different shapes. Let's look at other ways we can describe and measure an object. We can look at how tall an object is. This is called the *height*. We can also look at how long an object is. This is called the *length*.

Example: Trace the lines with your finger to tell which one shows the whale's length and which shows its height.

think! Can you think of another way we can measure this whale? Yes, we can tell how much it weighs! That is called the weight of the object.

PRACTICE: Now you try

Use red and blue crayons to draw lines to show the length and height of each object on the next page. Draw the red line to show the length. Draw the blue line to show the height.

Describe Objects

Morgan is holding her favorite teddy bear. In what ways can she measure her teddy bear? Show your work and explain your thinking on a separate piece of paper.

ACE IT TIME!

Math Vocabulary
- length
- height
- measure

	How many more?	yes	no
Did you find the question?		○	○
Did you circle helpful numbers and words?	② in all	○	○
Did you use pictures, counters, or numbers to help you solve?	2 apples	○	○
Can you explain your thinking in words?		○	○

MATH ON THE MOVE

Find different objects around the house that can be measured in length and height. Talk about how you can do this for each object.

CCSS.Math.Content.K.MD.A.1

Unit 7: CORE Measurement and Data Concepts

Compare Objects

UNPACK THE STANDARD
You will compare the length, height, and weight of objects.

LEARN IT: You can tell if an object is taller or shorter than another just by looking at them. You can also tell if an object is heavier or lighter than another object by feeling them.

Example: Look at the pictures of the giraffe and the bird. Use what you see to describe the size of the animals.

think! We can see in the picture that the giraffe is bigger, or taller, than the bird. But which animal do you think weighs more? Imagine picking up each animal. Which one is heavier?

The giraffe is **taller** than the bird.

The bird is **shorter** than the giraffe.

The giraffe is **heavier** than the bird.

The bird is **lighter** than the giraffe.

PRACTICE: Now you try

Look at the pictures on the next page. Answer the questions.

Compare Objects

1. Circle the animal that is taller. Draw an X on the animal that is shorter.

2. Circle the creature that is heavier. Draw an X on the creature that is lighter.

Anthony looked at the picture on the right. He thinks a zebra is lighter than a toucan. Do you agree with him? Why or why not? Show your work and explain your thinking on a separate piece of paper.

Math Vocabulary

heavier
lighter
taller
shorter

	Did you find the question?	*How many more?*	yes no
	Did you circle helpful numbers and words?	② in all	yes no
	Did you use pictures, counters, or numbers to help you solve?	 2 apples	yes no
	Can you explain your thinking in words?		yes no

Compare the weight of objects around the house. Pick them up (if they are not too heavy) and tell which object is heavier. Which is lighter?

CCSS.Math.Content.K.MD.A.2

Unit 7: CORE Measurement and Data Concepts

Classify Objects

UNPACK THE STANDARD
You will sort objects based on their shape, size, and color.

LEARN IT: You can put objects together in a group based on how they look. This is called *sorting*. You sort by color when you put all objects of the same color together in a group. Or you can sort all of the objects that are the same shape together. You can also sort objects by their size.

Example: Look at the shapes below. Sort them by color, shape, and size.

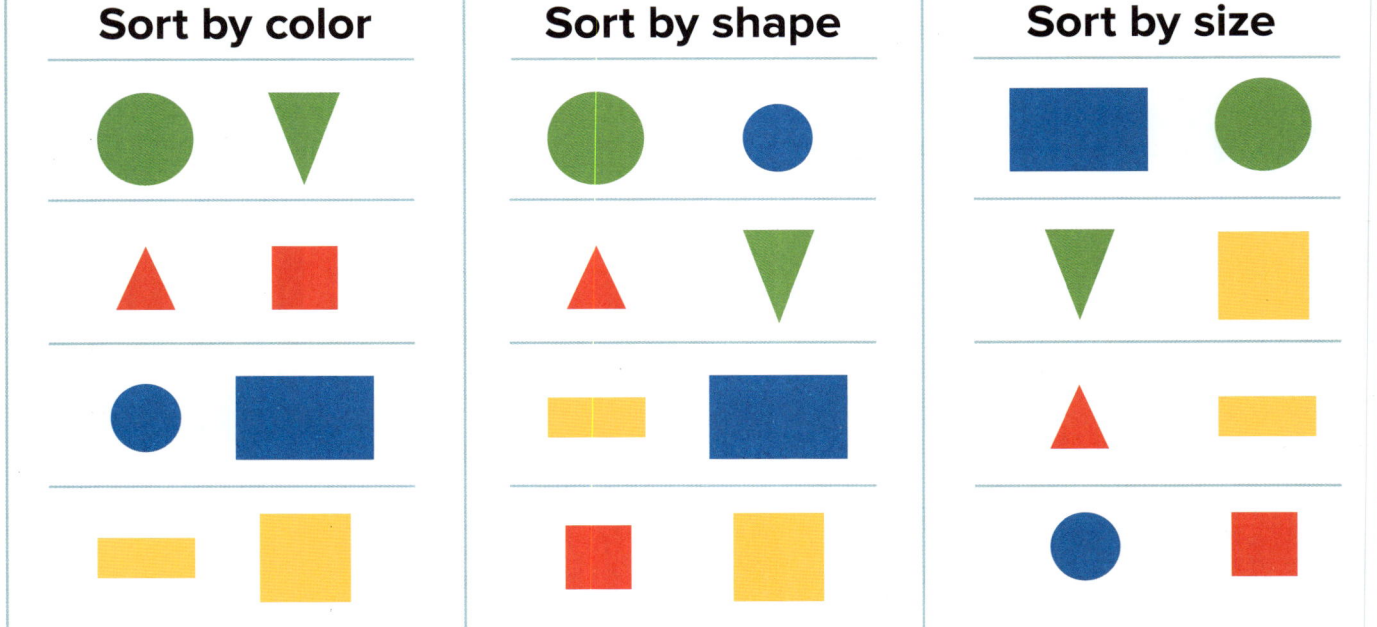

PRACTICE: Now you try

Sort the pictures into the groups shown on the next page. Draw each object in the correct box. Color to match!

Classify Objects

Sort by color	Sort by shape	Sort by size

Amir looked at the set of shapes shown here. Do you think the shape Amir drew goes with the group? Why or why not? Show your work and explain your thinking on a separate piece of paper.

Amir's shape

ACE IT TIME!

Math Vocabulary
- group
- sort
- color
- size
- shape

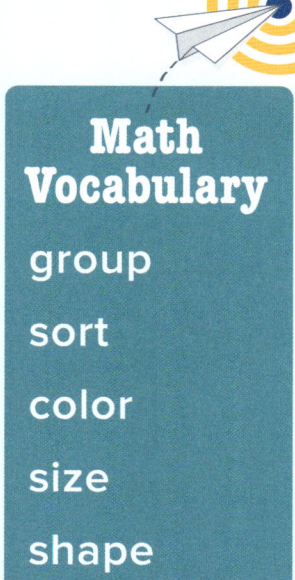

	How many more?	yes	no
Did you find the question?		○	○
Did you circle helpful numbers and words?	② in all	○	○
Did you use pictures, counters, or numbers to help you solve?	2 apples	○	○
Can you explain your thinking in words?		○	○

MATH ON THE MOVE

Help with the laundry! Can you find all the ways to sort the socks and other clothes in your family's laundry?

REVIEW

Stop and think about what you have learned.

Congratulations! You have finished the lessons for Units 6 and 7. You have learned about shapes. You can build shapes from other shapes, and describe the position of objects. You can also describe objects based on their length, height, and weight. You know how to sort objects by their shape, size, and color.

Now it's time to show your skills. Solve the problems below! Use what you have learned.

Activity Section 1

1. Name the shape. Count the sides and the vertices.

   Number of sides: _____

   Number of vertices: _____

   Remember, "vertices" means corners!

2. Name the shape. Count the sides and the vertices.

   Number of sides: _____

   Number of vertices: _____

3. Tell how the shapes are alike and different.

   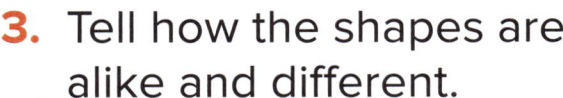

4. Name the solid. Can it stack, slide, or roll?

Stop and Think! Review   **Units 6–7**

5. On a separate piece of paper, describe the position of the solids.

6. Combine the shapes to make a rectangle.

Activity Section 2

1. Circle the snap cube train that is longer.

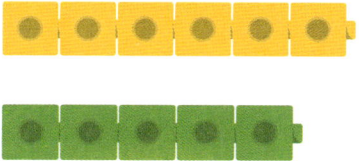

2. Circle the snap cube train that is shorter.

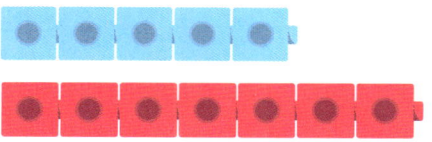

3. Circle the stack that is taller.

4. Circle the stack that is heavier.

5. Think of 3 different ways you can sort these objects. Draw the objects in your new groups on a separate piece of paper.

UNDERSTAND

Stop and think about what you have learned.

Use what you know about two- and three-dimensional shapes to solve the riddles below.

Activity Section

Who am I?

1. I am a shape with 4 sides that have the same length.

2. I am a shape with 0 sides. I am round all the way around!

3. I am a solid that can stack. I have 6 flat surfaces.

4. I am a shape that has 6 sides and 6 vertices.

5. I am a solid that has 2 flat surfaces. I can roll if you lay me on my side!

6. I am a solid that is shaped like a ball.

7. I am a shape that has 3 sides and 3 vertices.

8. I am a shape that has 4 sides and 4 vertices. Only my opposite sides are the same length.

DISCOVER

Stop and think about what you have learned.

You can find shapes in the world around you.

Activity Section

Look in the picture below. Use the key to color each shape.

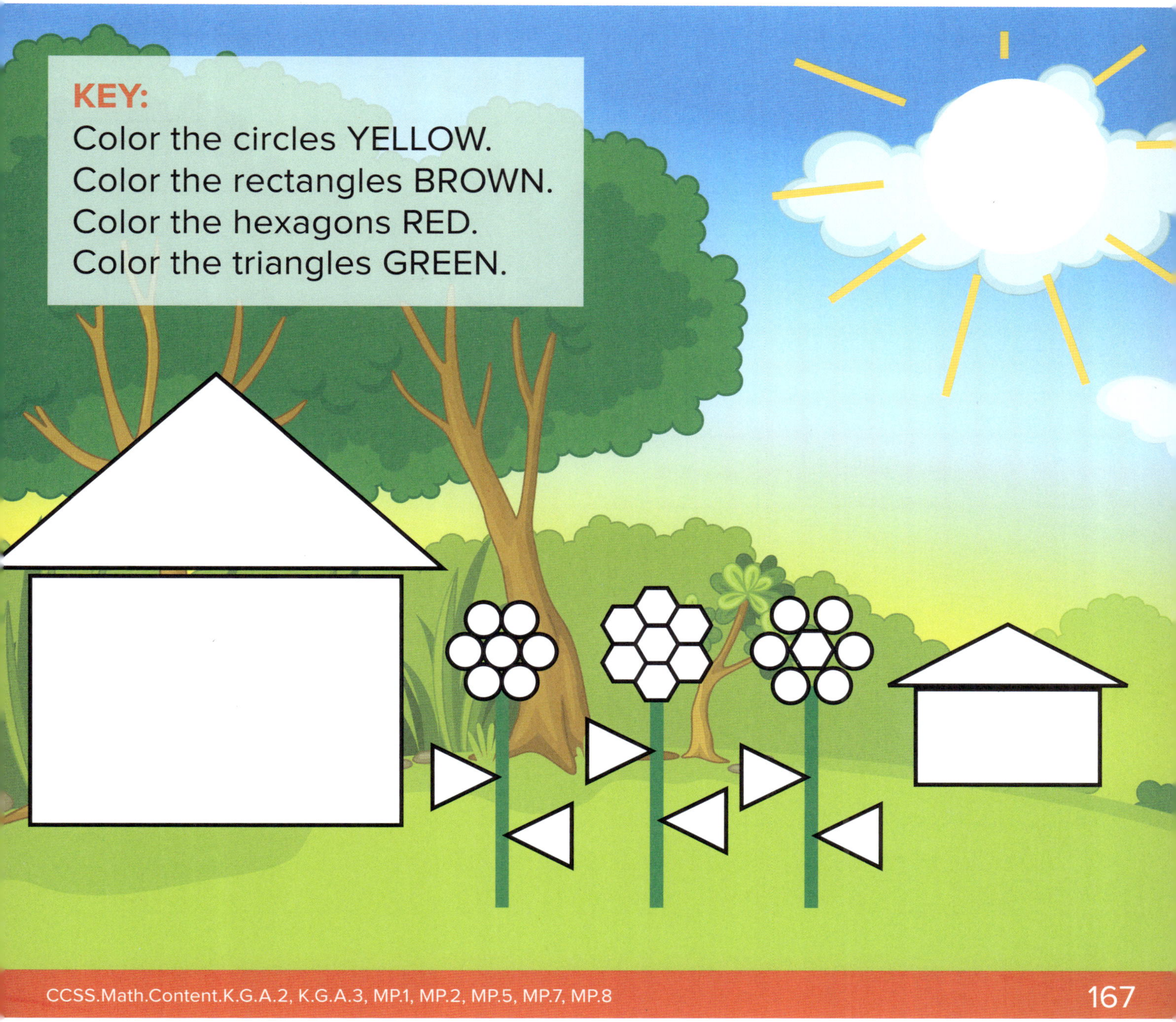

KEY:
Color the circles YELLOW.
Color the rectangles BROWN.
Color the hexagons RED.
Color the triangles GREEN.

Number Practice

Practice writing your numbers from 0 to 20.

0 1 2 3 4 5 6 7 8 9

10 11 12 13 14 15

16 17 18 19 20

Answer Key

English Language Arts

Unit 1: Learning to Recognize Word Sounds

Lesson 1—Understanding Rhyming Words

Page 16. Activity 1: bee/tree, truck/duck, dog/frog; Activity 2: 1. sun; 2. cake; 3. toy; Activity 3: pet/wet

Lesson 2—Understanding Sounds of Syllables

Page 17. Activity 1: flower, wagon; Activity 2: turtle/2, sheep/1, squirrel/2

Lesson 3—Understanding Onsets and Rimes

Page 18. Activity 1: A. st; B. fl; C. dr; Activity 2: bad/sad, fish/wish, miss/kiss

Lesson 4—Understanding Phonemes in CVC Words

Page 19. Activity 1: A. a

Page 20. Activity 2: /b/ /uh/ /s/, bus; /k/ /a/ /puh/, cap; /h/ /eh/ /n/, hen

Lesson 5—Making New Words

Page 21. Activity 1: A–C. bug, hug, rug; Activity 2: 1. a; 2. C. u; 3. fun

Unit 2: Learning to Recognize Words

Lesson 1—Learning Consonant Sounds

Page 23. Activity 1: door/dress, mouse/man, pony/penny; Activity 2: boy, basketful, bunnies

Lesson 2—Learning Long and Short Vowel Sounds

Page 24. Activity 1: A. if

Lesson 3—Recognizing High-Frequency Words

Page 25. Activity 1: are, you, to; Activity 2: my, The, is

Lesson 4—Words that Sound the Same

Page 26. Activity 1: i/a, a/i, e/o; Activity 2: A. get; B. let; C. met (order can be swapped)

Unit 3: Fluency: Read with Purpose and Understanding

Lesson 1—My Pet Zet

Page 29. Guided Questions: 1. C; 2. the vet; 3. Drawings should show a turtle stuck in a net.

Lesson 2—Ted

Page 31. Guided Questions: 1. C; 2. B; 3. C

Unit 4: All About the Senses

Lesson 1—Your Five Senses

Page 36. Learning About the Details: 1. eyes, ears; 2. B; 3. (2,3,1); 4. C

Page 37. Finding Nouns and Verbs: Activity 1: 1. circle/hear, underline/dog; 2. circle/see, underline/fish; 3. circle/feel, underline/sun; 4. circle/smell, underline/flower; Activity 2: Answers will vary. Sample: flowers, smell/I smell the flowers.

Page 38. How to Make Plural Nouns: Activity 1: 1. foxes; 2. trains; 3. boys; 4. potatoes; Activity 2: bushes, bench, noses, flea

Page 39. Using End Punctuation: 1. (?); 2. (.); 3. (?); 4. (!)

Page 40. Learning About Prefixes and Suffixes: 1. un; 2. re; 3. ful; 4. ed

Unit 5: Energy

Lesson 1—Sound Energy

Page 44. Main Topic and Key Details: 1. B; 2. C; 3. B; 4. B

Page 45. Pictures Help You Understand the Text: 1. Answers will vary. Sample: instruments that make sound or make music, things that make sound; 2. A; 3. A

Page 46. Practice Writing Upper- and Lowercase Letters: Dd, Cc, Bb, Tt, Jj or Pp, Ss, Ww, Ff, Oo; Circle: baby, siren, whistle

Page 47. Sort Objects: Fire engine, Firecrackers, Jackhammer, Horn

Lesson 2—Heat Energy

Page 49. Making a Connection: 1. Our body makes heat like the sun; 2. A; 3. Popsicle; Circle: pan, lightbulb; Underline: sun, fire

Page 50. What Are the Parts of a Book?: Front Cover; Title Page; Back Cover; 1. Lisa King; 2. Susan Coons

Page 51. Compare and Contrast Articles: Sample Answers: They both talk about energy. One talks about heat energy the other about sound energy.

Page 52. Prepositions: 1. in, 2. on, 3. down, 4. along

Page 53. Words with Many Meanings: 1. Do you like to bowl? 2. The duck is pretty. 3. My dad wears a tie. 4. Tree bark is rough. 5. She saw a bug. 6. We write with a pen.

Answer Key

Stop and Think! Units 1–5 Review

Page 56. Activity 1: Ff, Tt, Bb, Mm

Page 57. Activity 2: 1. front; 2. behind; 3. between; 4. around; 5. through; Activity 3: in, in, in, by, under

Page 58. Activity 4: Student should draw a square around the tent, camper, sleeping bag; Circle: fire, binoculars, flashlight, lantern; Underline: Don't feed the bears, trails, arts and crafts, lake, compass

Stop and Think! Units 1–5 Understand

Page 60. 1. B; 2. A; 3. B; 4. C

Page 61. 5. C; 6. C

Page 62. 1. A; 2. C; 3. C; 4. A

Unit 6: Nursery Rhymes and Poetry
Lesson 1—Mary's Lamb

Page 68. Understanding the Key Details: 1. C; 2. B; 3. C; 4. Children should tell the events of the story in the order in which they occur.

Page 69. Ask Questions About Unknown Words: 1. A; 2. C

Page 70. Recognizing Poems: Answers will vary. Sample: I see flowers on my bed. I taste something good to eat.

Page 71. Practice Writing Upper- and Lowercase Letters: Ll, Ss, Hh, Gg

Page 72. Short Vowel Sounds: u/hug, e/bell, a/cap, o/log, i/fish, o/bow

Page 73. Opposite Words: Opened, Empty, Cold

Unit 7: Fables
Lesson 1—The Ant and the Dove

Page 77. Main Characters, Settings, and Events: 1. Dove, Ant; 2. B; 3. B; 4. B; 5. If you help others, others will help you.

Page 78. Pictures Help You Understand the Story: 1. B; 2. C

Page 79. Ask Questions About Unknown Words: Activity 1: B; Activity 2: 1. river; 2. stone; 3. flutter

Page 80. Recognize Complete and Incomplete Sentences: Underline/Ants can make anthills. Underline/She stops to pick flowers. All other sentences are incomplete and should have a line through them.

Page 81. Using End Punctuation: 1. (.); 2. (?); 3. (!); 4.(!); 5. (?); 6. (.); 7.(.); Using Capital Letters: 1. Riding; 2. You, I; 3. On, I; 4. We; 5. I

Page 83. Understanding Question Words: 1. Where; 2. Who; 3. What; 4. How; 5. Why; 6. Which; Become a Good Speller: cat

Page 84. 1. sun; 2. boat; 3. fish; 4. net; 5. moon; 6. stars

Page 85. Real-Life Connections: Activity 1: slimy-worm, cold-ice cream, bright-sun, colorful-flowers; Activity 2: 1. slimy worm; 2. cold ice cream; 3. bright sun; 4. colorful flowers

Page 86. Shades of Meaning: Students will correctly act out the action words listed in 1–4.

Stop and Think! Units 6–7 Review

Page 88. Activity 1: 1. How; 2. Why; 3. What; 4. Where; Activity 2: Underline: The wolf is mean(.); The sheep are sleeping(.); When are they coming home(?); Help, I see a wolf(!); Students should circle: i/I; the/The; w/When; i/I

Page 89. Activity 3: 1. (!); 2. (.); 3. (?); 4. (!); Activity 4: two, fan, ant, hat; Activity 5: Students will correctly act out the words.

Stop and Think! Units 6–7 Understand

Page 91. Activity 1: C; 2. B; 3. The wolf was going to eat Little Red Riding Hood.

Page 92. 4. A; 5. Events should be numbered in order of how they occurred in the story 3, 1, 4, 2; 6. middle; 7. B; 8. A

Page 93. Activity 2: Red Riding Hood is a story about the danger of talking to strangers. Mary's Lamb is a nursery rhyme about a lamb being at school. Both of the stories are about girls. Both have animals in their stories.

Page 94. Activity 3: 1. walk; 2. eyes; 3. flowers; 4. noise; 5. hungry; 6. ran

Answer Key

Math

Unit 2: CORE Counting and Number Concepts (Numbers 0–10)

Explore Numbers 1–10
Page 107 Practice: Now you try
1. 3
2. 5
3. 6
4. 2

Ace It Time: The second set of lunchboxes has seven. (Student should circle the second set and should verbally explain how he or she knows.)

Count 0–10
Page 108 Practice: Now you try
1. 3
2. 8
3. 5
4. 0

Page 109
5. 7, 8, 9, 10
6. 6, 7, 8, 9, 10

Ace It Time: There are 10 fish in the tank. I know, because I counted on from 1 to 10. I touched each fish as I counted.

How Many?
Page 110 Practice: Now you try
1. 6
2. 8
3. 10

Page 111 Ace It Time:

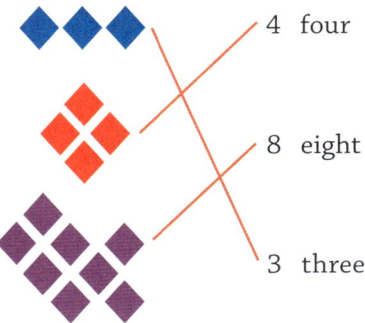

I counted 3 objects in the first group, 4 objects in the second group, and 8 objects in the third. Then I drew a line to match the numbers to each group.

Greater Than–Less Than–Equal To
Page 113 Practice: Now you try
1. 3, 5 (Student should circle the group of 3)
2. 8, 7 (Student should circle the group of 7)

Ace It Time: Ally's Shells: 4; Shane's Shells: 5. Shane's shells are the bigger group. 5 is greater than (or more than) 4.

Compare Numbers
Page 114 Practice: Now you try
1. 3
2. 9
3. 6
4. 2

Page 115 Ace It Time: Sam has more flowers. Sample explanation: Jane has less than 7 flowers, but more than 5. Jane has 6 flowers. Sam has 8 flowers. Sam has more flowers because 8 is more (or greater) than 6.

Unit 3: CORE Counting and Base-Ten Concepts (Numbers 11–19)

Break Apart Numbers
Page 117 Practice: Now you try
1. 17
2. 14
3. 18
4. 16

Ace It Time: Zach can break apart the number 16 into one group of 10 and 6 more ones.

Count 11–19
Page 118 Practice: Now you try
1. 12
2. 17
3. 11
4. 16

Page 119 Ace It Time: Anna counts 15 books. I counted 15 books, 10 on the top shelf and 5 more on the middle shelf.

Count On
Page 120 Practice: Now you try
1. [12], 13, 14, 15, 16, 17, 18, 19
2. [15], 16, 17, 18, 19
3. [17], 18, 19

Answer Key

Page 121

4. 19
5. 13, 14, 15, 17, 18
6. 15, 16, 17, 18
7. 14, 15, 16, 18
8. 17, 18, 19

Ace It Time: Luis is not correct. He does not count on from 11 correctly. He swapped 14 and 15. He should say "11, 12, 13, 14, 15, 16, 17, 18, 19."

Match Numbers and Names

Page 122 Practice: Now you try

1. Draw a line to 17.
2. Draw a line to 13.
3. Draw a line to 11.
4. Draw a line to 15.

Page 123

5. 16
6. 14

Ace It Time: Student should draw 12 soccer balls or 12 circles because she counted 12 soccer balls.

Stop and Think! Units 2–3 Review

Page 124 Activity Section 1

1. 8
2. 6, 7, 8, 9
3. 10
4. 7
5. 4 5 (Student should circle the group of 5.)
6. 6 8 (Student should circle the group of 6.)

Page 125

7. 4
8. 7

Activity Section 2:

1. 15
2. 14
3. 13
4. 18
5. 17, 18
6. 15, 16, 17, 19
7. 16, 17, 18, 19
8. 14, 16, 18
9. 18
10. 12

Stop and Think! Units 2–3 Understand

Page 126 Activity Section

Kate's page has 13 stickers. It has 10 ones and 3 more. Lee's page has 14 stickers. It has 10 ones and 4 more. Lee has more stickers.

Stop and Think! Units 2–3 Discover

Page 127 Activity Section

1. 7 (Student should draw 7 balloons, or circle representations.)
2. 6 (Student should draw 6 balloons, or circle representations.)
3. Andy has more balloons, because 7 is more than 6.

Unit 4: CORE Addition and Subtraction Concepts

What Is Addition?

Page 129 Practice: Now you try

1. 2 and 2 is 4.
   2 + 2 = 4

Ace It Time: 4 children were on the swings, because 1 child and 3 more is 4. 1 + 3 = 4.

Practice Adding up to 5

Page 130 Practice: Now you try

1. 2 + 1 = 3

2. 3 + 2 = 5

Page 131

3. 4 + 1 = 5

4. 2 + 3 = 5

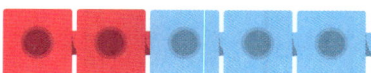

Ace It Time: They have 4 games all together because 2 + 2 = 4.

Make a Ten

Page 132 Practice: Now you try

1. Student should draw 2 squares, or cubes. 8 + 2 = 10
2. Student should draw 3 squares, or cubes. 7 + 3 = 10
3. Student should draw 4 squares, or cubes. 6 + 4 = 10
4. Student should draw 5 squares, or cubes. 5 + 5 = 10

Page 133

5. Student should draw 6 squares, or cubes. 4 + 6 = 10
6. Student should draw 7 squares, or cubes. 3 + 7 = 10

Answer Key

7. Student should draw 8 squares, or cubes. 2 + 8 = 10
8. Student should draw 9 squares, or cubes. 1 + 9 = 10

Ace It Time: You would need to add 10 snap cubes, because 0 + 10 = 10. Zero means there is nothing in the group.

What Is Subtraction?
Page 134 Practice: Now you try
1. 2
2. 1

Page 135 Ace It Time: Izzy has 1 bracelet left because 4 take away 3 is 1. 4 − 3 = 1.

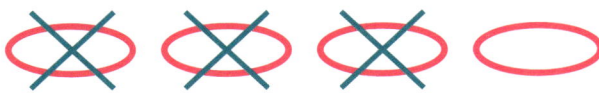

Practice Subtracting with Numbers 0–5
Page 136 Example:

$$5 - 3 = 2$$

Page 136 Practice: Now you try
1. 1
2. 2
3. 3
4. 1
5. 1
6. 3
7. 3
8. 1

Page 137 Ace It Time: A.J. had two pieces of watermelon and he ate both of them. He has none or 0 left. 2 − 2 = 0.

Unit 5: CORE Counting and Number Set Concepts (Numbers up to 20 and Beyond)

Count Objects up to 20
Page 138 Practice: Now you try
1. 7
2. 16
3. 9

Page 139
4. 20

Ace It Time: No the picture does not show 20. The second ten frame is not full; it is one less. It shows 9, making 19 in all.

Count to 50 by Ones
Page 140 Practice Now you try
1. Student should circle 25, count on to 50, and draw a box around 50.

Page 141
2. Student should circle 39, count on to 50, and draw a box around 50.

Ace It Time: Hailey made a mistake in her counting. She left the number 48 out of her counting order! 48 should come after 47.

Count to 100 by Ones and Tens
Page 142 Example:

1	2	3	4	5	6	7	8	9	(10)
11	12	13	14	15	16	17	18	19	(20)
21	22	23	24	25	26	27	28	29	(30)
31	32	33	34	35	36	37	38	39	(40)
41	42	43	44	45	46	47	48	49	(50)
51	52	53	54	55	56	57	58	59	(60)
61	62	63	64	65	66	67	68	69	(70)
71	72	73	74	75	76	77	78	79	(80)
81	82	83	84	85	86	87	88	89	(90)
91	92	93	94	95	96	97	98	99	(100)

Page 142 Practice: Now you try
1. 10
2. 20

Page 143
3. 30
4. 40
5. 50
6. 60
7. 70
8. 80

Ace It Time: The next two numbers will be 90 and 100. I know because I counted by tens. There is a pattern with the numbers counting by ones with a zero on the end: 10, 20, 30, 40, 50, 60, 70, 80, 90, 100!

Stop and Think! Units 4–5 Review
Page 144 Activity Section 1
1. 4 and 3 is 7
   4 + 3 = 7
2. 5 and 4 is 9
   5 + 4 = 9
3. 2 and 6 is 8
   2 + 6 = 8
4. 5 + 5 = 10
5. 7 + 3 = 10
6. 5 − 4 = 1

Answer Key

Page 145

7. 6 − 3 = 3

8. 7 − 7 = 0

Activity Section 2

1. 20
2. 20
3. Students should circle the numbers 36, 48, 63, 79, and 90 on the chart and count on out loud to 100.
4. 30
5. 60

Stop and Think! Units 4–5 Understand

Page 146 Activity Section

Student should fill in the missing numbers on the hundreds chart in the following order:

5, 14, 27, 28, 33, 46, 60, 62, 63, 78, 81, 99

Stop and Think! Units 4–5 Discover

Page 147 Activity Section

Student should circle ten groups of 10 and write that there are 100 gumballs in the jar.

Unit 6: CORE Geometry Concepts

Name that Shape

Page 149 Practice: Now you try

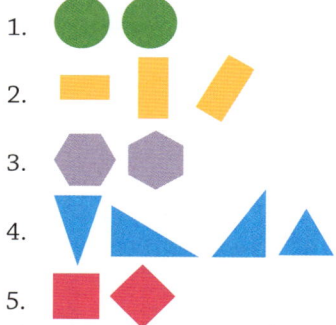

Ace It Time: Kyra is thinking of a hexagon. A hexagon is a shape with 6 sides and 6 corners.

Compare Shapes

Page 150 Practice: Now you try

1.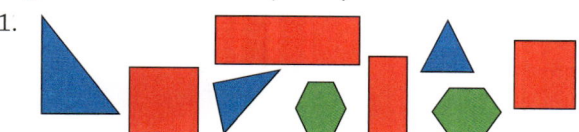

Page 151

2. ALIKE: both are two-dimensional flat shapes, both have at least 4 sides, both have at least 4 vertices
DIFFERENT: one is a hexagon, one is a square, hexagon has 6 sides and vertices, square has 4 sides and 4 vertices

3. ALIKE: both are two-dimensional flat shapes, both have at least 3 sides, both have at least 3 vertices
DIFFERENT: one is a rectangle, one is a triangle, rectangle has 4 sides and 4 vertices, triangle has 3 sides and 3 vertices

Ace It Time: A square and a rectangle both have 4 sides and 4 vertices. A square has all 4 sides that are the same length, or equal, and a rectangle does not. Its opposite sides are equal.

Cylinder, Cone, Sphere, and Cube

Page 153 Practice: Now you try

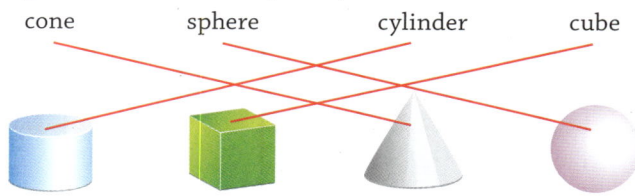

Ace It Time: Answers will vary. Some spheres Jeremy could have collected could include any kind of balls, an orange, peach, plum, a gumball, etc.

Build Shapes

Page 154 Practice: Now you try

1.

Page 155

2.

3.

Ace It Time: I can combine two trapezoids like this to make a hexagon. I know this is a hexagon because it has 6 sides.

Where Is It?

Page 156 Practice: Now you try

1. Student should circle and name the cube. Student should draw an X on and name the square.

Page 157

2. Student should circle and name the hexagon. Student should draw an X on and name the circle.

Ace It Time: Abby is in front of Brent. Brent is behind Abby and in front of Carlos. Carlos is behind Brent.

Answer Key

Unit 7: CORE Measurement and Data Concepts
Describe Objects
Page 159 Practice: Now you try

1–3. Student should say and draw the red and blue lines for length and height.

Ace It Time: Morgan can measure how long her teddy bear is. This is the length. She can measure how tall her teddy bear is, or the height. She can also measure how much her teddy bear weighs.

Compare Objects
Page 161 Practice: Now you try

1. Student should circle the lion and put an X on the monkey.
2. Student should circle the elephant and put an X on the butterfly.

Ace It Time: Student should not agree with Anthony because a zebra is heavier than a toucan. It is bigger and weighs more.

Classify Objects
Page 163 Practice: Now you try

Sort by color	Sort by shape	Sort by size
Student should draw all the red objects.	Student should draw all the roses.	Student should draw all the large objects.
Student should draw all the yellow objects.	Student should draw all the stars.	Students should draw all the small objects.
Student should draw all the green objects.	Student should draw all the fish.	

Ace It Time: Yes, Amir's shape can be grouped with the shapes shown. All the shapes in the group are sorted by shape. They are all triangles. The size and color of the triangle does not matter.

Stop and Think! Units 6–7 Review
Page 164 Activity Section 1

1. Rectangle; 4 sides; 4 vertices
2. Hexagon; 6 sides; 6 vertices
3. They are both two-dimensional shapes with sides and vertices. The square has 4 sides and 4 vertices. The triangle has 3 sides and 3 vertices.
4. Cone. It can slide and roll when it's on its side.

Page 165

5. The cylinder is beside (or next to) the cube. The cube is below the sphere. The sphere is above the cube.
6.

Activity Section 2

1. Student should circle the longer train of 6 cubes.
2. Student should circle the shorter train of 5 cubes.
3. Student should circle the taller stack of 7 books.
4. Student should circle the heavier stack of 10 books.
5. Student should sort the objects by color, size, and shape. For example, all the green objects together, blue objects together, and yellow objects together. Then, all the books together, all the notebooks together, and all the pencils together. Lastly, they can sort all the large objects together, and all the small objects together.

Stop and Think! Units 6–7 Understand
Page 166 Activity Section

1. square
2. circle
3. cube
4. hexagon
5. cylinder
6. sphere
7. triangle
8. rectangle

Stop and Think! Units 6–7 Discover
Page 167 Activity Section

Student should color the picture following the colors listed in the key.

GRADES 2–6 TEST PRACTICE for Common Core

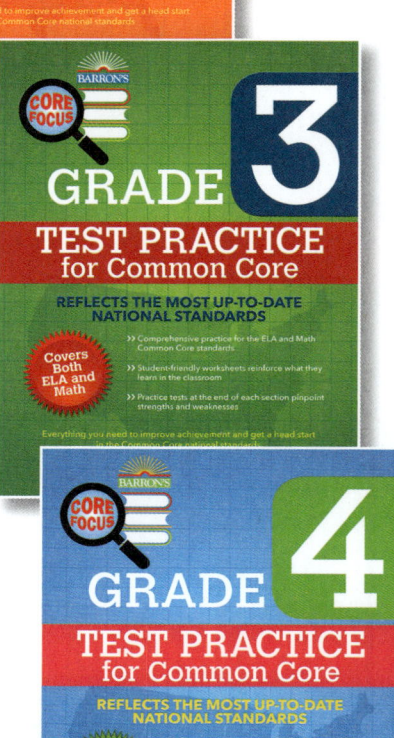

With Common Core Standards being implemented across America, it's important to give students, teachers, and parents the tools they need to achieve success. That's why Barron's has created the *Core Focus* series. These multi-faceted, grade-specific workbooks are designed for self-study learning, and the units in each book are divided into thematic lessons that include:

- Specific, focused practice through a variety of exercises, including multiple-choice, short answer, and extended response questions
- A unique scaffolded layout that organizes questions in a way that challenges students to apply the standards in multiple formats
- "Fast Fact" boxes and a cumulative assessment in Mathematics and English Language Arts (ELA) to help students increase knowledge and demonstrate understanding across the standards

Perfect for in-school or at-home study, these engaging and versatile workbooks will help students meet and exceed the expectations of the Common Core.

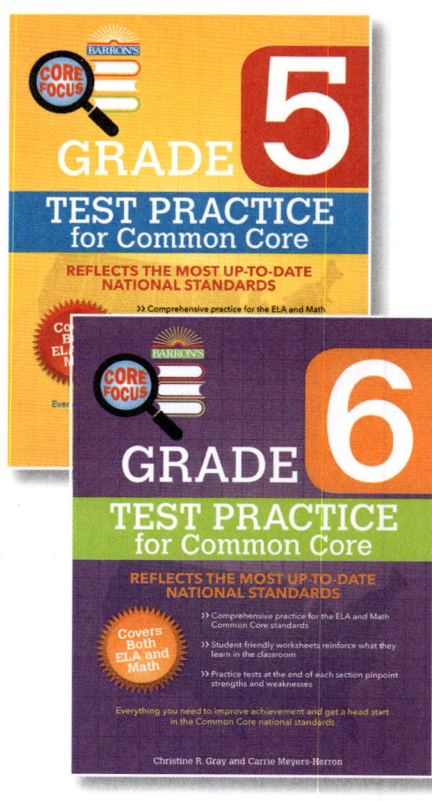

Grade 2 Test Practice for Common Core
Maryrose Walsh and Judith Brendel
ISBN 978-1-4380-0550-8
Paperback, $14.99, Can$16.99

Grade 3 Test Practice for Common Core
Renee Snyder, M.A. and Susan M. Signet, M.A.
ISBN 978-1-4380-0551-5
Paperback, $14.99, Can$16.99

Grade 4 Test Practice for Common Core
Kelli Dolan and Shephali Chokshi-Fox
ISBN 978-1-4380-0515-7
Paperback, $14.99, Can$16.99

Grade 5 Test Practice for Common Core
Lisa M. Hall and Sheila Frye
ISBN 978-1-4380-0595-9
Paperback, $14.99, Can$16.99

Grade 6 Test Practice for Common Core
Christine R. Gray and Carrie Meyers-Herron
ISBN 978-1-4380-0592-8
Paperback, $14.99, Can$16.99

Barron's Educational Series, Inc.
250 Wireless Blvd.
Hauppauge, N.Y. 11788
Order toll-free: 1-800-645-3476

In Canada:
Georgetown Book Warehouse
34 Armstrong Ave.
Georgetown, Ontario L7G 4R9
Canadian orders: 1-800-247-7160

Prices subject to change without notice.

Coming soon to your local book store or visit www.barronseduc.com

(#295 R11/14)